To the most

Soul & Mother

Renu.

2018

The POWER OF EGO

Master Your Life!

Rémi Meyer

<u>DISCLAIMER</u>

TABLE OF CONTENTS

What is an "EGO"?

"Ego" means "the self " or the "I." It is the psychic apparatus driver as well as the director of the movie of our lives. To be able to develop an optimal understanding of the ego, we must first dissect our psyche, which should be followed by a close study of each of its aspects through the lenses of several great minds in psychology, psychoanalysis, philosophy, sociology, anthropology, and biology. Those scholars dedicated their entire life to the research, analysis, and explanation of this sophisticated complex domain of the human science.

Each chapter of the book will independently address one of the essential ingredients of our character and personality. These are usually expressed outwards as a unity via our individual egos. As each chapter prudently unfolds, the correlations between all of them will gradually emerge to you – the reader. These ingredients are the fundamental aspects that construct our psyches and include tendencies, desires, emotions, feelings, instinct, intelligence, will, habit, memory, imagination, perception, sensation, attention, language, and many more.

Therefore, the process of acquiring an insight and a deeper understanding of these aspects, their functions, and their interrelationships is exactly like putting together the pieces of a puzzle. While solving a puzzle, you need each and every piece to form the image, just as you would need all the parts for the seamless and functional operation of a machine.

Therefore, it is up to you – the reader – to collect these essential pieces or parts and assemble them accurately, so you can clearly see what makes you tick, thus enabling you to see your own non-physical picture.

Moreover, as the Swiss psychiatrist and psychoanalyst Carl Gustav Jung once said, **"The psyche is the greatest of all cosmic wonders and the "sine qua non" of the world as an object. It is in the highest degree odd that Western man with a very few – and ever fewer – exceptions, apparently pays so little regard to this fact."**

"Swamped by the knowledge of external objects, the subject of all knowledge has been temporarily eclipsed to the point of seeming nonexistence."

"The Ego is the hidden force, that stands between you and the Universe."

Rémi Meyer

"There will always be a reason why you meet people. Either you need them to change your life or you're the one that will change theirs."

Angel Flonis Harefa

ACKNOWLEDGMENT

This work would not have been possible without experiencing the horrendous maternal emotional abuse, which I faced during my growing up years. These adverse circumstances planted in me a seed for an unquenched passion to understand the human psyche. Yet, despite all the pain I endured, I am grateful to my mother. She is a good woman, however, she was not shown better and neither did she know better.

Thank you, Divine Lord for guiding me towards a path in life, which invited me to grow in so many innumerable ways that I will forever be thankful to you. You, Lord, granted me with this fiery desire to share this beacon of light with everyone who needs it.

At the outset, I would like to express my gratitude to the many friends who were with me throughout the completion of this book, and also to all those with whom I had the pleasure to discuss the content of the chapters. In addition, and for all of you who read the first draft of the manuscript to provide their feedbacks have been an essential step in this journey. Thank you for endorsing my desire to spread this knowledge for the service of others and believing in me. This work would not have been intrinsic without each of these encouragements and the fate that led me to study psychology under the mentoring of a truly superb and dedicated psychology professor, "Nahiya Abou Mourhi." She made the subject a beautiful story about mankind and she always reminded us that, **"Curiosity is characteristic of a vigorous mind."**

"So that my soul will sing praises to You and not be silent. O Lord, my God, I will thank You forever."
(Psalms 30:13)

INTRODUCTION

Why Write This Book?

I have a burning desire to share the knowledge, wisdom, and experiences that have contributed to the construct of this book. Over years, several books have helped thousands of people including myself to live life increasingly being consciously aware of the individual psyche. Being self-aware can greatly enrich our life experience. Therefore, after 20 years of studying and researching the domain of psychology and its repercussions in metaphysics seeking to understand the human psyche, I wanted to compile comprehensively in one single book the imperative foundations for anyone seeking a guide to their inner life. A true teacher does not really teach you, as it is not possible to see you as inherently separate from him/her. Correspondingly, throughout this book, I am simply using knowledge to help you reflect back your own inner knowing, which is an aspect of our intuition (that I will elaborate in detail on throughout the book) and to remind you of the vastness of your essence.

Why Share Knowledge or Wisdom?

The great philosopher, Mahatma Gandhi, once said, **"You must be the change you want to see in the world."** Thus, it is imperative that for change to happen in the world, it must initiate from within each one of us.

We all know material resources are limited, but the innate resources like knowledge and wisdom are unlimited. We currently base the majority of our existence on material growth, which is why our consciousness remains in a limited and slow progression. However, when our development is underpinned by knowledge, then the consequent growth is unlimited. For example, if I share with you my knowledge, then it gets multiplied by two because you then possess the same knowledge as I do. And congruently if I share it with a hundred people, it gets multiplied by a hundred.

However, if I give you a product or a material object, say 50 USD. This 50 USD is not mine anymore, and I have as a result decreased my financial capacity by exactly 50 USD. But when I give you knowledge it still remains in my possession equally. When I gave you the 50 USD, it was a quick transaction and the result is directly reflected in your hand or bank account. However, the resource of knowledge cannot be traded it in such a fast manner; and it is a gradual process, which takes time to be communicated in its true essence. However, undoubtedly, the shared knowledge will eventually multiply, subject to the number of people who learn it!

It is your individual decision, to choose what to take on from this book. I cannot teach anyone anything; however, **I can indeed make you think.** The majority of the knowledge and wisdom as described in the book is age-old and referenced from minds that hundreds and thousands of years ago dedicated their entire lives to understanding the human psyche. Some of them are Jung, Descartes, Husserl, Delay, Mauss, Condillac, Pradines, Compte, Bergson, Watson, Socrates, Freud, Lagache, Aristotle, Plato, and several others. I want to bring into focus, the significance of understanding the components of the psyche by detailing all of the aspects through the time-tested research and studies, which were conducted by these great minds in psychology, psychoanalysis, philosophy, sociology, anthropology, biology and metaphysics. Therefore, without the understanding of your own psyche, it would not be possible to rationally discern your own self, nor can you commence an inward journey of self-discovery. It would be like you trying to fly a commercial airplane without any license or training.

We can definitely try to steer clear of the metaphysical correlations to stay focused on scientifically verifiable data; though, inevitably and organically it will lead us to open the Pandora Box for many metaphysical repercussions pertaining to life and the soul. For, when an individual is confronted with the paradox of wanting a purpose while concurrently thinking that mankind existence is meaningless, cognitive dissonance will certainly occur. Throughout history, this enigma has led many to scope for spiritual and religious guidance, thereby challenging science, as it failed to answer the existential questions such as: Why or What am I?

Therefore, my advice is to test-drive this entire bank of constructive information derived from great minds and identify what works best for you.

Hillel the Elder a Jewish religious leader once said, **"If I am not for myself, who will be for me? If I am only for myself, what am I? And if not now, when?"**

Why Should you Invest in Understanding your Psyche and Its Repercussions?

Consider: You wake up one morning and decide to quit smoking or quit drinking alcohol or maybe to address the excessive shopping habit emptying your bank account.

Now, on the first day, you successfully succeed in overcoming the adverse habits.

However, on the second day, post a very stressful working shift, the smoker along with the drinker surrender to their urges, with the objective to cope and forget about his/her rough day. And, even the person who did not want to spend excessively on shopping just bought a jacket, which was on sale.

Thus, we can safely infer that most often than not, we end up breaking promises we make to ourselves. Are we, then, hypocrites? Why are we unable to stick to our rational thinking or decisions? What are the reasons behind such conduct?

No, we are not hypocrites; and neither are we unable to adhere to our rational thinking or decisions. The underlying reason for this peculiar behaviour is the association of the majority of our actions with our instinctive and subconscious needs ingrained at a deep level with previous experiences, formed during our childhood.

Therefore, to strengthen our core towards addressing shortcomings, like giving in to the subconscious, as demonstrated in our irrational reactions, we need to address these concerns at the root-level. It is imperative to realize that majority of our actions and reactions are merely coping mechanisms to the deeper level of the suppressed self, which is seeking recovery.

You need to heal the roots, i.e. the origin of all behaviour to heal the consequent patterns, emerging in your psyche. **Once you succeed in doing so, you become proactive and not reactive; i.e. the cause and not the effect. Consequently, you start to happen to life instead of life happening to you.**

This raises the fundamental question; as to why would you do that? You may state that you are comfortable with your status quo and do not perceive the requirement of any impending healing or recovery. Well, think again.

We all drift into an "automatic" mode of reactions, which is based purely on our subconscious programming. The subconscious has no choice but to run as default, which is simply its job for our psyche. Similar to the heart's job is to pump blood by default to the entire body. Thus, all the negative things that we spot in others or the world are merely a reflection of our own shadows (our subconscious). The subconscious contains our own bespoke versions of the truth, which is formed through our social, parental, educational and environmental conditions, which constitute in fact, our limitations too. **Because each time we come up with a conclusion about a subject we are limiting ourselves from other possibilities.** Irrespective these limiting aspects are born from our present condition – or that of our past that continues to linger in our subconscious – our ultimate responsibility is to uncover these aspects. Thus, to make a change we must willingly choose to re-program our subconscious in a new direction to transition away from the old programming that may not be serving us anymore.

""The art and science of asking questions is the source of all knowledge.""

Thomas Berger

The Anagogical Question: "Why"?

"Why" is a very intriguing and powerful word, composed of only three letters. It has been observed that number 3 has underpinned the minds of many legends. Correspondingly, great minds, including Nikola Tesla, who discovered wireless electricity, presented quite unique habits. Tesla used to walk around the block three times before entering a building, and he lived in hotel rooms with numbers that were divisible by three, also he would always perform tasks and experiments in sets of three. He once said, "If you only knew the magnificence of the 3, 6 and 9, then you would have a key to the universe." Therefore, there is definitely an exclusivity surrounding the number three.

In nature, this number is very important. Evidently, everything that needs to be done in balance requires the inclusion of three fundamental components. Number one, on its own, is singular and thus does not provide room for anything else; it is all oneness. Number two introduces a distinctive one and then one other. Number three introduces a new element, which is the mediator and thereby creates harmony in the Trinity.

To further elaborate on this concept, let us consider a simple example. For a light bulb to produce light, it requires a positive and negative charge as well as a resistance, which is the filament. Consequently, sans the filament that pushes back on the negative and positive charge to create light, the direct connection between the two polarities would create a big spark of light, which would last for only a few seconds before ending up in darkness. Humans represent that filament and notably, the only difference between a 100 or 200-Watt lamp is the strength of this filament.

Let us review few other examples, too. A vehicle requires three things: a skeleton, an engine, and a driver. Our psyche also presents three components expressed as a unity: The id, the ego, and the super-ego, which is discussed in detail, later in the book. In addition, three is the number, which is inherently related to time, i.e. past, present, and future; and congruently most things constitute a beginning, middle, and an end.

Have you ever wondered why children are full of questions, especially with those that start with the word **why?**

This is corroborated by the quote from the English write Samuel Johnson, "Curiosity is one of the permanent and certain characteristics of a vigorous intellect."

As adults, with our conditioned psyche, we constantly ask the questions with tags like who and how, and less of why, because we are programmed to accept things without questioning them. However, who and how deal with the symptoms, while why addresses directly the cause. Furthermore, mankind have used the why primarily to project it towards the external things in the world. Also, throughout time, our intelligence has been mainly directed and exercised towards the external things, which is clearly indicative that we still have not acquired the habit to purposefully align and exercise it towards an inward journey.

When children ask why, it stems from their innate curiosity to decipher and make sense of the surrounding world, to understand it, and further obtain explanations of their operative environments. The first time, I took my niece to swim in the sea, she was three years old, and since, she was used to only swimming in pools, her first two questions were: Why there is salt in the water? Who put it in?

I burst with joy at the beautiful innocence and rationale of the questions, children ask. As adults, we often fail to realize the capability of children and all their efforts comprehensively aimed towards trying to understand the world. Therefore, everything we say to them is constantly contributing towards the construction of their own reality.

"All matter originates and exists only by virtue of a force... We must assume behind this force the existence of a conscious and intelligent Mind. This Mind is the matrix of all matter."

Max Planck

The Imminent and Important Question:

Why Do We Exist?

The most probable outcome is that you may never discover why you exist, and what the purpose of your life is **if you choose to do nothing about it.** It is very easy to get caught in living a facile life and miss out on the real reason of our lives. Several theories have attempted to convey to us the origins and story of life. However, the approbation of these theories is subject to our current level of consciousness. The more we expand and open our individual minds to the vast potentials or possibilities, the more we are able to receive. These imperative questions will help us on our journey inward to try to understand "why" we are here now. And there are no parallels, for each one of the 7.4 billion human beings on earth will have their own unique story to tell about "why I am here."

In many places, and for the majority of people, it is a taboo to talk about spiritual knowledge. Irrespective, if the conversation pertains to subjects involving harmless opinions or facts, which otherwise we may even find helpful and could rationally agree with - assuming we had not been conditioned to operate in a certain way. That said, for the purpose of asking why, I would share with you the most common stories taught about life. Notwithstanding, if you are a believer or an atheist, an understanding of my intention to include these stories at the start of this book, will gradually emerge - so that you can begin questioning **why?** And then you can journey inward in search of your own answers.

The Genesis creation story belongs to both Judaism and Christianity. On the first day, God created light, separated darkness from it, and called it day and night. On the second day, God created the firmament, to separate the waters from the waters and called it the sky. On the third day,

God created the land and gathered the waters, calling the dry ground land and the gathered waters seas. On the fourth day, God created the sun, the moon, and the stars to give light upon the earth, as well as signs to mark the seasons, days and years. On the fifth day, God created every living creature in the seas and all winged birds and then blessed them to multiply. On the sixth day, God created the animals, Adam and Eve in his own image, blessed them and gave them all creatures to rule over and care for. Finally, on the seventh day, when God finished his work of creation, He went up to the heavens to rest.

Likewise, the creation narrative as found in the Quran, states God created everything from nothingness. He created the earth, the skies, and the entire cosmos. Following which, from water, he made all the creatures that walk, swim, crawl, and fly. Then God created the angels, the sun, the moon, and the stars to move in the universe. Afterwards, God created Adam from earth and water and breathed life into him. He then created Eve out of a rib from Adam. Then, God poured down rain on the earth for it to sprout the soil with vegetation and fruits, olive, palm, and grass. According to the Quran, in addition, the earth was to be inhabited by several other creatures, like the Jinn, created from fire without smoke, and that they existed before God created mankind.

The latest scientific creation narrative evidence the persistent attempts, over the last century, of several scientists to figure out how the first life originated on earth. These researchers have even tried recreating this "Genesis Moment" in their labs, with the purpose to create brand-new life from scratch. The large Hadron Collider in Switzerland is built to understand the "Higgs Boson," also known as "the God Particle." However, till date, there has been no known occurrence of anybody being able to manage it. Yet, the researchers are confident of following the right track. In fact, as a race, we have progressed excessively since the first basic theory of evolution of humans from apes. Notably, while none of the other races has executed such a huge leap of evolution, it is one species of the ape genus, which evolved as mankind!

Lastly, let me share with you the Kabbalah narrative of decoding what it is written in the Torah. Specifically, the Torah contains 5 books (Genesis, Exodus, Leviticus, Numbers and Deuteronomy) from the same book Christianity calls the Old Testament and is written in Biblical Hebrew and Aramaic, the language of Yeshua (A.K.A the Christ). Prior to the creation or existence of any matter, there was only Light – the Divine – which indeed is this galactic endless intelligence, presented with a desire to share and experience itself. In absence of anything else, beyond the Light, the Divine decided to create an empty space within itself to create a vessel, i.e. a giant soul. This vessel was created to receive the Light and, therefore, it contained the properties of the Divine. Hence, it presented the inherent desire to co-create and halt the process of simply pure receiving. And, this is where the vessel chartered itself into individuals, i.e. Lights or souls to create our living reality, impacted by self-discovery or self-awareness. This is the "big bang" moment according to what science claim to be the beginning of everything. Correspondingly, at this juncture, the mighty Divine Light concealed itself from mankind behind multiple curtains of physical and metaphysical realms called "Sephiroths," as named by the Kabbalists. Their purpose is to assist mankind to reveal the Light of the Divine through overcoming their nature, elevating matter and conquering the darkness of the physical reality.

Now, which one of the above narratives resonates with you? And more importantly, ask yourself: **why?**

In addition, many other cultures have also written about the creation. These descriptions, clearly evidence that these quest stories, few among many, are aimed at discovering our ultimate origin. These are the narratives of our origin, which led to the creation of struggles amongst individuals, and elaborated and broadened imaginations, as well as brilliant creativities. As we dig deep to decode each of these stories, we conclude they all convey an identical sentiment and are simply creative variations of the same reality. However, each story follows a diverse perspective construct, subject to individual consciousness level. Also, the coding is underpinned by the individual developmental time frame impact.

"I acknowledge the privilege of being alive in a human body at this moment, endowed with senses, memories, emotions, thoughts, and the space of mind in its wisdom aspect."

Alex Grey

We Exist With a Body, Our Vessel: The Moment an Ovum Meets a Sperm

Only one out of the millions of sperm constituting the semen, fertilize an egg. In fact, the science tells us that only one sperm is even allowed to fertilize the egg. And post fertilization, in case any lone sperm breaks through the egg's wall, the egg starts to release a special hormone that prevents any other sperm from further entering the egg. Therefore, the union between that egg and the fertilizing sperm results in the specific construct of each individual body. Notably, from the millions of potential sperm, there is only one that breaks through and fertilizes the egg. The reasons as to why that specific sperm managed to enter the egg are still not known by our science.

This particular moment, i.e. the union of the sperm and egg, marks the initiation of the human embryo creation in the womb of the mother. Also, this moment is the primary determinant point as regards to your specific traits as a human being. These determination factors are based on the expression of approximately 80,000 different types of genes. Specifically, humans have 46 chromosomes, 23 from the sperm and 23 from the egg. Therefore, during conception, your father and mother equally contribute to the construct of your 46 chromosomes. However, regardless the transference of the exact same chromosomes from parent to child, their quality can subsequently either be diminished or improved, depending on our individual experiences. Therefore, the individual qualities become altered according to our life choices. Your genes change and adapt to the surrounding environment, identical to your continual change and adaptation to the environments.

The exquisite design of your vessel, i.e. your human body contains the entire genetic evolution of your ancestors, both paternal as well as maternal. Hence, it naturally requires, without any doubt, full respect, love, care, and understanding. Your DNA contains the genetic code – the blueprint – as regards to the built of every individual part of your body. However, DNA is also subject to several environmental influences including society, diet, mindset, chemical exposure, ancestry, and education. These influences present potential significant effects on the body, leading to beneficial DNA mutations that enable organisms' adaptation to the changing conditions. However, this is a gradual process occurring over several generations. The American poet, memoirist, and civil rights activist, Maya Angelou, correspondingly, once said, **"I come as one, I stand as ten thousand."** You may even stand as hundreds of thousands or even millions. What in fact matters is that you are the genetic evolution of everyone who came before you!

DNA is Not Just the Blueprint of Life but Also the Carrier of Trauma

Recently a paradigm-shifting study titled, "Soma-to-Germline Transmission of RNA in Mice Xenografted with Human Tumour Cells: Possible Transport by Exosomes," was conducted by Cossetti et al. (2014). This, and an experiment performed at Emory University in Atlanta, Georgia, suggests that the fears experienced by a parent can be inherited by their offspring through the chromosomes of a species' germline cells, i.e. through DNA changes in the sperm or egg. Correspondingly, a systemic observation of the life of holocaust survivors, evidence an inadvertent transference of the trauma after effects to their children and grandchildren; and relatively, the effect of it through the lives the Jewish people can be safely inferred. For example, they are extremely community-focused, virtually govern themselves, and care strongly for the needs of their members. Likewise, the Jewish communities remain one of the few modern world societies, still closed to the outsiders. This can confidently be attributed as a direct result of a self-preservation mechanism triggered due to their traumatic history. These findings and observations evidence "trans-generational epigenetic inheritance", which means that the environment can affect an individual's genetics that can be passed on the subsequent generations. Another simpler example is from humans living in high latitudes, who present fairer skin, through the evolution of many generations, owing to the lack of sun exposure. Thus, we are directly responsible of the individual experiences of our physical bodies and ancestry that we pass on to our children, including the environment we provide to them. Therefore, we are responsible for the legacy we leave behind to our children.

Some scientists suggest that similar phenomenon of emotional trauma influences anxiety and addiction in humans. However, some researchers are skeptical of these findings because of the lack of an identified specific biological mechanism explaining the phenomenon. However, not finding a mechanism does not imply that the phenomenon is incorrect. It simply is indicative of our limited understanding within the medical community as regards the human body as well as its psyche or metaphysical aspect. The moment scientists begin to commonly acknowledge that we are not just a biological vehicle but an energy structure as well; humanity will make a major leap towards emerging the supreme race we are meant to be.

The human body is designed to navigate the natural laws of the universe and experience life with everything that we intend to desire. Necessarily, we must not discard the function of DNA within the body, i.e. being an inner space for a memory bank. Since every part of the body contains DNA, every part develops its own memory, yes! As much as the mind!

To discover the self, it is imperative to dive into all of our diverse aspects. It is important to dissect our psyche to determine respectively the inherited and acquired characteristics, which helped condition our psychological, sociological, philosophical, and spiritual lives. All of this sheds an insight into your psyche construct and the subsequent effect on you. However, the majority of us do not realize that most of our daily actions are subconscious. Numerous cognitive neuroscientists have conducted studies that similarly reveal the subconscious nature account of 95% of our cognitive activities (decisions, emotions, actions, and behaviors); while the remaining 5% are generated in a conscious manner. The subconscious part constitutes our memory bank, where we store our beliefs, memories, suppressed emotions, trauma, and automated behaviors. Singularly through self-actualization and observation, you will come to understand that everything in this universe, including your psyche with your body, is seeking harmony and balance; also this exchange of energy is never a one-way street.

To become more conscious of one's self, we need to dig into our shadows, i.e. our subconscious mind and the so-called blind spots. These constitute the aspects of our being; such as the behaviors, attitudes, habits, triggers, beliefs, emotions and feelings. Yes! Elements we did not know that we had! Yet we act instinctively upon them, and it all happens totally subconsciously, with a complete exclusion of the intervention from our conscious mind. We need to be in a state of observing the ego and its resistances, patterns, and repetitions. We also need to cultivate confidence, practice letting go of anything that does not serve us any longer to free the psyche and enable it to follow its authentic path to achieve fulfillment.

Regarding spirituality, it is important to highlight I am not referring to a specific religious system, or to any type of a cultural philosophy. Rather, I am talking about the individual actions that you do to take care of yourself. This quest, therefore, leads you to the discovery of another dimension of you, a luminous, endless, and powerful part of your being. In fact, when you are connected with your spirituality, it transforms your inner state to joy, freedom and equanimity. It also completely transforms the way the body feels, as it acts as a catalyst to elevate your essential state of being.

C H A P T E R   0 1 :

PSYCHOLOGY AS A SCIENCE

All sciences are characterized by their objects, their methods, and their laws. The object of a science is the totality of the phenomena of facts constituting the domain of the studies, observations, hypotheses, experiments, laws, and conclusions. The method of a science refers to a set of particular rules governing the operations of thought in the study of its object. Finally, a law of a science is an expression of a constant and necessary relationship between two or more phenomena, and these relationships are often expressed using mathematics and statistics.

Given this notion of science, in psychology we are faced with a twofold problem:

1. Does psychology constitute a proper and formal object? Or is it, in fact, a part of another science, like biology or sociology?

2. In the affirmative case, does psychology present particular methods and tangible results or laws?

To answer these questions, we need to conduct a detailed and relevant review of the different definitions accorded to psychology throughout history and identify the ideal definition as per the requirements of scientific objectivity.

Is Psychology a Science of the Soul?

Before we review the history, we must first examine the exact nature of the word and its connotations. The word psychology is etymologically formed from two Greek words translated as "science of the soul." The first word, ψυχή (psūkhē), means "life" or "breath," and the verb ψύχω (psukhō, "to blow") includes derived meanings such as "spirit" or "soul." The second word, λόγια (logia), means "study of" or "science."

Indeed, such expression is contradictory and unfortunate. A "science" is the positive study of facts, defined in experiences and the respective governing laws; while conversely, the notion of the soul is metaphysical. We observe in it the supernatural and the free will principle, immortal from the spiritual and moral life. Based on this understanding, clearly, the soul cannot be the object of a "science." Therefore, we question whether or not psychology is a science of consciousness or of "the inner life," because for a "science" to exist, we must attribute to it a specific, concrete object, and a method. The object of this psychology thus is "the inner life," rather than the soul or consciousness, since it escapes measurement, while "the inner life" is a concrete and living world of memories, images, dreams, feelings, ideas, and more. Another, more relatable term for this method is "introspection."

Introspection refers to the inner observation of our states of consciousness. In some ways, it is like a dimensional time-travel tool to our past, which thereby enables us to examine ourselves.

Basically, it is the knowledge of oneself by oneself. Each of us individually can observe our own inner life. This method thus indicates a sort of contemplation, self-analysis, meditation, and reflection of consciousness on itself, which thereby supposes a true doubling of the self: A "Me" observer and an "I" observed. This essentially makes classical psychology a psychology of perspective in the first person. Specifically, a perspective in the first person presents the relation between a phenomenon and a subject (a person), in a scenario where the actual subject is able to comprehend the phenomenon.

The introspective method can be linked to Socratic thought "Know thyself," and underpinned by one of Socrates's well-known quotes: **"The unexamined life is not worth living."**

Socrates lived in 399 BC and was a Greek philosopher that taught both Plato and Aristotle; the famous students who laid the very foundations of Western philosophy.

What is Introspection?

"Can you look at something so completely, that the space between you – the observer – and the thing observed, disappears?" said Jiddu Krishnamurti, an Indian mystic, speaker and writer.

Introspection involves the conscious and rational examination of oneself, and correspondingly, 'knowing thyself' is the fundamental demand of spirituality from the followers. However, this raises precisely the concern, if attaining knowledge of thyself and self-objectivity by oneself is possible and fruitful? Am I two entities, a "Me" observer and an "I" observed, i.e. in other terms the observer is the observed. Thus, is it possible that maybe I am more than two entities in one body? Moreover, if the modality of introspection could constructively result in the development of this knowledge, then this matter, in fact, constitutes an authentic science.

To establish an understanding of introspection, we need to consider the criticisms offered by several sociologists and psychologists.

The first criticism that addressed introspection belongs to the French philosopher Auguste Comte, and continues to be famous till the present times: "Introspection does not realize the conditions of a good observation, so that a good accurate observation is possible, it is necessary that the subject who observes and the object to be observed are very distinct, just as one cannot simultaneously be at the window and watch oneself passing in the street. In the same way one cannot simultaneously live and watch oneself live, think and watch oneself think."

Thus, in accordance with Auguste Comte, introspection, does not fulfill the conditions of duplication for these previously mentioned reasons. Therefore, Comte accords no place in his classification of sciences to psychology and reduces the psychological problems either to biology or sociology.

Firstly, it is clear that introspection cannot lead to the acquisition of higher intellectual functions knowledge such as judgment and reasoning. This is because the very exercise of its operations mobilizes thought, which then is no longer available for the intellectual function of observation. A thinking individual cannot divide himself or herself into two beings, i.e. one that would argue and another that would reason. In an analogous manner, this observation could not adhere to the phenomenon of non-intellectual psychology, like emotion or passion. For example, when I am very emotionally moved or angry, this heightened emotional state, limits my capability of performing intellectual reasoning.

Thus, it can be safely inferred that we cannot live and observe oneself concurrently. Correspondingly, we could agree and recognize that we can live first and then observe. Introspection then becomes retrospection, which consists of remembering and revisiting the past moments. This reasoning leads us to question if this method serve as a means to know oneself objectively.

Retrospection does, indeed, realize the duplication of the subject and the object, but this is achieved through the use of memory. However, the memory is never faithful, as it can be deformed, impoverished or enriched. This malleability of the memory can be attributed to its mode of selection, which is based on the individual's orientation of values, attention and current situation. The process pertains to the contemplation of memories from our past, which are beyond our control today. However, we can validate that looking back into the past does not require the reflexive process that the "self" would impose, despite it involving one's own experiences.

When we introspect, we are at the verge of improving the self, despite that this may not lead to an objective knowledge of oneself - which is because it is always accompanied by a desire for self-justification or self-accusation. I do not know myself as I am, but as I would like myself to be. For these reasons, introspection also fails to present the serenity required for a scientific method. Henri-Louis Bergson, one of the most well-known French philosophers, presented a famous criticism of traditional introspection, wherein he substituted an original form of introspection.

Traditional introspection is an operation of intelligence but, according to Bergson, as an instrument to observe the inner life, intelligence is inept, as it has first and foremost exclusively exercised itself over the external things in the world, i.e. on the physical reality. Intelligence can explain, analyze, and measure it. However, intellectual processes applied to the inner life can only result in its deformation. It is not possible to halt the states of consciousness through their analysis or measurement, as they form a continuous current that presents a constant transformation and enrichment. Attributing to all these reasons, Bergson replaced this intellectualist introspection with another form of knowledge, which he termed "intuition."

Manly Palmer Hall, an astrologer and mystic asserts, "The heart and mind must be brought into perfect equilibrium before true thinking or true spirituality can be attained. The highest function of the mind is reason; the highest function of the heart is intuition, a sensing process not necessitating the normal working of the mind."

Intuition is a kind of empathy, which one uses to attempt an access to the very heart of the object to coincide with it, and this coincidence is a direct contact. Intuition is, therefore, a direct grasp of the inner life, which consequently projects a direct vision of the inner self by the inner self. This projected vision is subjective and singular and sans the need for a conscious reasoning. This intuitive knowledge appears to ideally align with the Utopians as it appears as scientific knowledge. Specifically, the concept of Utopianism tends towards the totalitarian thought-processes by seeking universal laws, which in turn, attempt to reduce either behavior or cognition to totally explainable processes. However, the ideology that we retain from Bergson's reflections is that the inner life is rebellious to analysis and measurement, and thus for this reason it cannot be classified as a science in the strict sense of the word.

Contemporary psychology pushes the criticism of psychology much further and goes so far as to refuse any reality of the "inner life" concept. Although, the very idea of an inner world possibly opposed to the outside world seems like fiction. Bergson is accused of projecting a specific belief in the reality of his inner world, considering the "states of consciousness" such as perception, memory, and emotion. For example, if I perceive a pot of flowers on my balcony, this perception does not pertain to an internal state; in fact, it is an act of my consciousness aimed at an object of the external world. Likewise, a recollection of a particular day from my vacation, is not a purely internal reality, rather it denotes an act of my consciousness' movement towards certain events occurring in my past. The same can be equally attributed to emotions and feelings.

Let me demonstrate the concept with another example; like, when I notice a stranger rushing towards me, I start to feel scared. Here, my fear appears not as an inner datum, but as an attitude in the presence of someone or could be something. Therefore, the data of my consciousness cannot constitute an inner life. However, conversely, according to the famous formula of Husserl, "Everything is consciousness of something." Thus, consciousness is intentionality, i.e. always directed towards something external to me. The fact is that consciousness is not a state but an act, i.e. a relationship between the subject and the object.

Are These Criticisms Really Decisive? Should we, Therefore, Reject Introspection?

It cannot be argued that this method is indeed difficult; on one hand, because of its spiritual and dynamic objectivism, which is in perpetual evolution, and on the other hand, because of the duplication. Of course, the spatial duplication of which Auguste Comte speaks is impossible, however the possibility of duplication in time cannot be ignored. A meticulous observation proves to us the impossibility of an individual to constantly control himself or herself through a reflection on his/her feelings and ideas.

The fact remains that irrespective of the magnitude and volume of difficulties we are forced to confront, introspection remains necessary and possible. While recognizing the challenges of introspection, one cannot overlook them. In alignment with the introspective point of view, subjectivity appears as essential psychologically, wherein the observation of consciousness by itself constitutes the practice fundamentals. Such is the opinion of Théodule-Armand Ribot: **"The method of inner observation is the fundamental method of psychology.**

Without introspection there will be no beginning for self-observation." This perspective reveals the necessity of this method as this autonomous reflection allows a person to reach and understand the psychic life nuances. Introspection presents prodigious outcomes, as all individuals with a desire to cultivate their minds can practice it; provided the occurring environment is beyond a consuming situation, i.e. external to emotional and intense conditions.

However, Ribot highlighted its insufficiency saying, "with it nothing ends." Correspondingly, introspection cannot suffice for the constitution of a scientific psychology culminating in laws and general objectives' knowledge. It is insufficient due to its confinement to the field of consciousness and ignorance towards subconsciousness. Thus, introspection does not reveal to us either the others or ourselves, because human life cannot be reduced to just consciousness.

This subsequently leads us to psychology in the second person, which consists of the knowledge of the other. Whereby, I aim or try to grasp the other intuitively (i.e. to understand that person by communicating with him/her from within), by addressing that person and calling him/her "You." The object of this psychology is the "You," and the method followed is either analogical reasoning or intuition.

By Analogical Reasoning

I know of others by comparing them to myself. My own experiences allow me to comprehend the attitudes adopted and presented by others. For example, I am very perceptive of my friend's emotions; and if I see my friend Sophia sobbing, I understand that she is deeply upset. I know from personal experience that I would cry in such a way when I am very upset. Similarly, I would guess her inhibition when seeing her blush, and also I would recognize her anger by observing her violent gestures.

Psychology in the second person can therefore be purely and simply brought back to psychology in the first person through the process of analogical reasoning. Although, initially, it does not seem imperative to go through reasoning to accord meaning to the attitudes and expressions projected by others. For example, a baby responds spontaneously to the smile of his mother. While the infant is unable to decipher any reasoning at that age, he/she still reacted, thereby demonstrating an understanding of this affectionate act. Therefore, no real analogy is apparent between the expressions of others as I perceive them and my own expressions, such as the ones I express with my own body.

Similarly, the analogy reasoning presupposes an accurate self-knowledge and also that this self-knowledge base serves as a reference to the knowledge of others. Such a position, as we have seen in analyzing the difficulties of psychology in the first person, is entirely gratuitous or simply not possible.

Finally, the researched criticisms evident on research review state that reasoning using analogy provides a subjective and an uncertain knowledge of others, and cannot be categorized as a scientific method.

By Intuition

As previously discussed intuition is the ability to understand something immediately, and instinctively, without presenting the need for conscious reasoning. Although, it is limited in certain aspects when it is employed either in a conflict situation or in a "sympathy or antipathy" scenario. Specifically, in these conditions it cannot provide an objective knowledge of others because the subject (a person) does not necessarily adopts a neutral attitude towards the other subject. Rather, the individual would project on the subject the individual feeling he/she feels towards them.

Hence, the discussion yields that psychology in the second person cannot ensure an objective knowledge of others as it is subjective, and is determined by the subject itself. Therefore, the book progresses to present and review a different approach.

Objective Psychology (A.K.A. Behavioral Science)

Difference Between Objective and Subjective Psychology

The purpose of subjective psychology is to study "the inner life," or conscience life, which offers methods based on the subjectivity of the person with the ability to utilize rational introspection, intuition, reasoning by analogy, and the communication of consciences.

Objective psychology does not have as objective to study the behavior of living beings. However, it uses the experimental methods, and can provide an empirical and objective knowledge of behaviors.

The Origin of Behavioral Science

The origin of behavioral science or objective psychology can be traced back to the beginning of the 20th century, with animal psychology research (the works of Piéron in France as well as by Thorndike and Köhler in Germany) and other research done in psychology laboratories. Today, objective psychology has evolved as a science, which offers a wide scope applicability to the studies of animals, children, mentally ill, and even the primal man.

Correspondingly, the American psychologist John Broadus Watson invented the term "Behaviorism" and established the psychological school of behaviorism that studies the psychology of behavior. However, the concept of behaviorism refuses to accord any significance to consciousness. Watson regarded it as an epiphenomenon (i.e. a secondary phenomenon added) and admitted that consciousness couldn't constitute an object of scientific study.

Therefore, as defined by Watson, behaviorism is the science of behavior, which is an external phenomenon with objectively observable set of reactions. An individual in response to stimuli would generate these reactions. While studying behaviorism Watson ignored the internal mental state of these individuals, and furthermore argued that it must be objectively observable from the external environment. In his opinion, the analysis of behaviors and reactions constituted the only objective method to develop an insight into the human actions.

A behavior is an automatic projection of a series of our reflexes and refers to an association, an addition, a simple chain of reactions, called reflex, which trigger each other. Scientifically, the term reflex refers to an automatic reaction, which is triggered by a stimulus. The impression of the external stimulus is first received by the nerve endings, which is then transmitted by the sensory nerves to the center of the central nervous system. From the nerve center, the response passes through the motor nerves that command the muscles to react.

The study of behavior, according to Watson, consists of establishing the relations that exist between the stimulus and the reaction. Thus, human behavior analogous to animal behavior, i.e. it is purely mechanical. Mankind thus is accorded the status of a machine according to the mechanistic behaviorism. However, a question would arise as a fallout of this principle wonder: If the stimulus and the reaction intersect in an automatically determined relationship, then how is it that two similar organisms (a person or an animal) react so differently to the same stimulus? For example, consider two dogs of the same breed; while one reacts by escaping, the other reacts by approaching to the same sound of bell. Watson responds to this objection by identifying this behavior with reference to the Conditioned Reflex Theory, as studied by Pavlov.

Pavlov's Famous Experiments

Ivan Pavlov a Russian psychologist found that a dog starts to salivate (an innate natural reflex) when presented with a piece of meat (a natural stimulus). He then coupled the presentation of meat with the ringing of a bell (an artificial stimulus). He found that, after repeated exposure to both, the dog began salivating when only the bell was rung. Consequently, salivation developed as a conditioned reflex. However, when another dog, external to the study was presented with only the artificial stimulus, no salivating occurred.

Watson explained that the different reactions of the two dogs to the same artificial stimulus presented evidence towards the different types of conditioning. The conditioning not only explains the behavior of animals but also the behavior of humans. Human behavior is, therefore, a sum of innate and conditioned reflexes, and correspondingly, "What we are is what we do and what we do is what the environment causes us to do," said Watson.

Criticisms on Mechanical Behaviorism by Neobehaviorism

Watson's viewpoint, however, is not acceptable because a living being cannot be categorized as a machine and thus, neither the stimuli nor the reactions can be described as physical objects. Therefore, stimuli are not objective in the same sense like a physical fact. According to behaviorism, the stimulus is objective, i.e. any object in the vicinity of an organism (a person or an animal) functions as a stimulant for that organism and automatically causes a reaction. However, experiments evidence that the same object can act as a stimulus on an individual and not on another. For example, the examination room is a stimulus for the candidates and not for a simple observer. Similarly, a forest projects a different stimulus for a hunter, a painter, a botanist, and two lovers.

Moreover, it is not the physical proximity of the object that constitutes it as a stimulus but rather its proximity to the psychological state of the individual, i.e. the interest it generates for the person. For an object to function as a stimulus, it must belong to the "umwelt" (a German word meaning "environment" or "surroundings") of the subject to its surrounding environment, and the world of its tendencies, needs, interests, and demands.

Finally, the reaction in fact, cannot be termed as automatic! According to behaviorism, the reaction automatically depends on the external stimulus. Correspondingly, experiments have shown that reactions are not passive because they are presupposed by a specific activity of the organism. Thus, they are not an automatic chain of reflex, but a creative synthesis capable of adapting to the spectacle to which it is finalized. A reaction is an adaptation to an end that is one of the aims desired from a living being.

Thus, the term Neobehaviorism defined behavior as a set of reactions developed as an adaptation to a situation. Behavior is no longer considered as an automatic chain of reflex but as a subjective response to a situation, which presents a particular meaning for the subject.

The merit of behaviorism projects a specific focus on the corporeal dimension, which has been long ignored by classical psychology (1ˢᵗ and 2ⁿᵈ person). Thus, mankind is no longer just a pure spirit, but rather a living organism with the constituents of a biological body and a psyche. Behaviorism also presents the merit of introducing measurements in psychology (such as tests and experiments), which are imperative for all sciences. However, it has been observed that the psychic facts most often resist measurement, particularly when it comes to the affective facts characterized by their subjectivity.

The psychic life constitutes a unity or a synthesis wherein the elements intersect and connect with one another. To measure these elements it would require an imperative process to separate them from each other's, thus, any measurement in psychology is artificial. Correspondingly, as a result, the scientists say, **"To formulate laws in psychology is to destroy psychology."**

Thus, in psychology analogous to all human sciences, one tends to replace the "knowing" by the "understanding." However, certainly, these remarks should not lead us to exclude experimental psychology and to deny the possibility of formulating certain laws in psychology: For example, the law of learning, of forgetting, and of sensation.

Furthermore, psychology is in fact, the science of conduct, which is presented in its current definition. The modern psychology of 21ᵗʰ century proposes it as a positive science aligned with both - the consciousness of an individual and its body – the biological, social, and historical dimensions. Likewise, Pierre Janet, a pioneering French psychologist, philosopher, and psychotherapist in the fields of dissociation and traumatic memory, states: "The psychic fact is neither corporeal nor spiritual, it takes place in the whole individual because it is only the conduct of this individual taken as a whole."

In the same perspective, Daniel Lagache, a French physician, psychoanalyst, and a professor at the Sorbonne University in Paris, defines conduct as: "The ensemble of organic motor, mental, and verbal operations, by which a personality in a particular situation tends to reduce the tensions that motivate it and to realize its possibilities." Clearly apparent from this definition, conduct is a global response of being in a given situation.

From the definition of Lagache, it is possible to extract the essential ideas that impact the comprehension of specific nature of conduct:

The word "ensemble" suggests the idea of unity or synthesis. However, it is a unity in a plurality and the elements that constitute our being, which merge to form the same identity. The word "operation" implies the dynamic nature of our psychic life and correspondingly, the elements constituting the set of operations, present a real interaction.

We Can Reduce These Operations to Two Categories

1. **Predominantly corporeal** – such as reflexes, instincts, habits, pleasures, pain, etc.

2. **Predominantly intellectual** – such as judgment, reasoning, images, memories, etc.

These two elements constitute the same unity to form our personality, which includes both: the innate and the acquired, the character and education, the individual and the social.

On a careful observation, it is apparent that our conduct presents the most often motivated aspect of us, which includes our tendencies, needs, and desires that appear to be the great motives pushing us towards action and knowing.

Methods in Modern Psychology

In consideration of the complexity and richness of any psyche, it is natural that the modern psychology would use multiple and diverse methods. This is analogous to the experimental introspection, which constitutes the study of the description given by the individual of his/her own states during a specific situation. Additionally, the modern psychologists use tests with the intended challenge to know and, when possible, to measure certain characteristics of the studied behavior. These tests claim to singularly isolate the ability to study all other innate or acquired factors.

Type of tests

1. The aptitude tests or objective tests, which seek to measure the aptitudes of a subject. These tests are used to measure intelligence, memory, speed of learning, technical skill, amongst other aptitudes. For example, the Binet-Simon test is used to measure the intelligence quotient (the mental age divided by chronological age is equal to the intellectual consciousness) using the following formula:

I.Q = (M.A/C.A) x 100

2. The Attitude tests or projective tests, which seek to reveal the affective structure of the personality. These tests are used to measure shyness, anguish, and emotions amongst other elements. For example, the Rorschach tests, where the subjects' perceptions of inkblots are analyzed.

The Value of These Tests

These tests offer the advantage of an objective and scientific knowledge since they allow an exact measurement and correspondingly render a great service in pedagogy and psychiatry.

However, they also present a disadvantage of the inability to reveal the different behavior patterns of a person in a concrete and natural situation, as against in an artificial and experimental scenario. Conversely, it is difficult to measure a natural aptitude by isolating it from the acquired knowledge and customs.

Example of types of test or methods:

- Interrogations, questionnaires, and surveys, applied in the field of social psychology.

- Methods in pathological psychology.

- Psychoanalysis, which is the most effective and excellent method of exploring the subconscious.

These methods underpin the origin of several branches in psychology such as animal psychology, child psychology, abnormal psychology, and comparative psychology. The latter constitutes the study of behavior or mental faculties and cognition of animals in order to determine the evolutionary relationships between species. While developmental, cognitive, and other forms of psychology focus primarily on the humans, and comparative psychology typically studies animals genetically related to humans.

Psychology has been observed to present itself in multiple aspects with different methods because its object (the psychic fact) constitutes the most complex part. Hence, the means of studying such an object must be widely varied. Correspondingly, the diverse conceptions of psychology and the various methods are not found to be mutually exclusive and in fact, they actually complement each other. In reality, the science of the inner life and the science of behavior, introspection, and intuition all can be categorized as clinical psychology. For instance, on one hand, it is scientific psychology; while on the other hand; it lends itself a mutual support. Thus, the different orientations of psychology are observed to be converging and complementary in nature.

Therefore, psychology is a science, but it diverse from the sciences of nature. It is a human science, the science of mankind - the science of committed and engaged spirit in the world; of a mind in sync with the totality of physiological, biological, historical, and social conditions.

Psychology is in fact, a science or a discipline that seeks to explain by appropriate methods all the phenomena that are difficult to explain.

CHAPTER 2

RELATION OF THE PSYCHIC FACTS TO THE ANATOMY-PHYSIOLOGICAL AND THE SOCIAL FACTS

In this study, it is imperative to explain the behavior of a living being. It no longer needs to be a mere description with references to biology (the consideration of the organisms and their functions) and/or to sociology (the social and historical environment where it behaves and where it is located). People, who study psychoanalysis, observe that physiological conflicts seem to result primarily from an opposition between the instinctive impulses sourcing from the organism, and the prohibitions transmitted by education that originate from society. Thus, psychology seems to need both biology and sociology in order to illuminate the object of its research.

Some of the psychologists and sociologists witnessed in the psychic fact a simple meeting point of the biological and the social aspects. This is corroborated by Auguste Comte, who, in his classification of science, accorded no place to psychology. The object of psychology is divided between two sciences: biology and sociology. According to Comte, a living being can be defined as an animal with history and similarly, all the possibilities of mankind are virtually inscribed in our organic structure.

However, such possibilities have been realized in accordance with historical events and the cultural environment. The place of our birth, presents our emergence into a certain state of civilization that marks our educational environment. Thus, attributing to these reasons, the human behavior is explained by the vast and diverse possibilities and tendencies of our animal nature specified by our individual social surroundings. When we grow up, our moral and ethical compass is almost entirely forged by our environment, and hence our actions are often a result of the validation from the society. Social psychology often considers the basic human need to fit in and calls this "The normative social influence." Thus, with this discussion, the significant impact of biological and social factors in our behavior is evident, which in turn, allows us to make an informed decision as to whether psychology retains some autonomy as regards to biology and sociology.

Relationship between Psychic and Anatomy-Physiological Facts

The level of behavior and intelligence is subject to the complexity of the nervous system. In vertebrates, for instance, the level of intelligence can easily be compared to the development of the brain. The intelligence of mankind has been studied and linked to the considerable volume of the cerebral hemispheres as well as to the interior of the brain, particularly the developments of the cortex.

Scientists have conducted expansive studies with the objective to clarify the correspondence between psychic life and cerebral functioning by locating the psychic function in certain parts of the brain. This theory, emerged at the beginning of the 19th century as a hypothesis and subsequently acquired scientific value after the observations of the French physician, anatomist and anthropologist Paul Broca. In April 1861, Broca presented to the society of anthropology the brains of a 50-year-old man who had died in his hospital service and for years had lost the use of speech. On conducting the brain autopsy of this sick individual, he found a lesion of the third frontal left convolution. Broca identified this location as the center of the articulation of language.

By studying the diverse lesions, the scientists have garnered excessive knowledge, towards assessing the precise location of the sensory functions and the motor functions. In addition, the scientists have determined the areas of the brain where the sensory nerves and the motor centers presenting movement control are located. During the course of these studies, it was found that a lesion of a motor zone causes paralysis. Moreover, a lesion of the so-called "psychomotor" centers provokes apraxia; in such cases, one does not get paralyzed, however, the individual loses the ability to recognize how to use objects. Correspondingly, when an individual presents the loss of the memory and the meaning of gestures, it is evidenced with a lesion of the sensory area that produces insensibilities. For example, a lesion of the visual area, in the occipital lobe causes blindness. Similarly, a lesion of a psycho-sensory area causes agnosia. Like in the case of a tactile agnosia, at the touch, the subject is incapable of recognizing a familiar object. Equivalently, the scientists have also learned that cerebral localizations are limited in scope. They correspondingly, identify the precise location of the elementary motor "sensory" functions, however it was impossible to assign a specific cerebral territory to a complex psychological process.

Kurt Goldstein, a German neurologist and psychiatrist, has conducted expansive studies to show that the brain functions as a whole. According to him, the least psychic activity tends to bring the entire brain into play and even further, the entire organism. Indeed, it is not possible to isolate the nervous system within the organism. Dr. Jean Delay, a French psychiatrist and neurologist, reminds us that the most elementary scale is in the center of the most complex. The functions of the nervous system depend on the chemical balance of the blood of its composition "in sugar, albumin, fat, minerals, acids and salt." Likewise, it is essential to accord a particular emphasis on the influence of the hormones secreted by the endocrine glands, and this is where we are able to identify the close relationship between the sexual instinct and the sexual hormones. For example, the adrenaline secretion by the suprarenal is an essential element of the functions of emotion. The deficit of the thyroid hormone is accompanied by a weakening of intellectual power. All these facts demonstrate the enormous importance of organic factors in the mental health and life of an individual.

Psychologists and physicians of the 19th century were largely influenced by the progress of cerebral physiology and by the discovery of localizations. However, this comprehension, subsequently led them to commit the error of limited scoping of these facts. Thus, they often interpreted them in a simplistic way, within the framework of a materialistic psychology, with the tendency to view human behavior as the mechanical result of organic functioning. The individual was no longer considered with the perspective of a living whole, but as a mechanism constituted of detached parts. Likewise, for the materialistic physician, the human body was simply a conglomeration of a brain, arteries, cells, and others. This evidences the dominant emergence of physiology over psychology.

Today, there has been a dynamic development in the psychology and the medical sector, which have brought to life the aspect of the concrete living subjects. The specific psychological point of view has emerged as being widely emphasized in the current medical system. It has been evidenced that a patient is better understood and cared for only when he/she is treated in the family conditions as well as in the social context and in reference to his/her personal history. There has been an evident transition in the principles underpinning the medical field from the 19th to the 21st century. At the end of the 19th century, while all the diseases were sought to be explained by an external microbial or toxic agent attacking organic mechanics, in the 21st century, the importance of purely psychic causes in the disorder of the organism itself, has been widely acknowledged. Extensive researches in the last few decades have introduced the clarity that several mental illnesses present no organic causes. The source of neuroses must be sought in psychological conflicts and the consequent findings are very remarkable. One such finding is that sexual behavior disorders rarely depend on a glandular disorder. For example, hormone-based treatments do not impact any change in the homosexuals into heterosexuals. Thus, psychoanalysis seeks to understand and restore sexual variations through uncovering subconscious conflicts, by reconstructing the patient's "unwell" history and by seeking out the distant influences impacting the construct of his/her affectivity.

Therefore, the explanation between psychic and physiological facts evidences a reversal without denying the influence of the organism on the psyche. In this description, the book aims to shed light on the influence of psychological conflicts on organic functioning.

The studies of certain functional disorders like asthma and digestive disorders present the pathogenic power of psychological conflicts on the body and this subsequently led to the formulation of psychosomatic medicine. Dr. Jean Delay writes that the great periods of suffocation of an asthmatic correspond largely with the separations of a loved one. Correspondingly, an individual suffering from a stomach ulcer would present a regular fluctuation of their stomach enzymes and acid levels. The psychosomatic process is easy to understand: A vivid emotion produces a hyper-secretion of the stomach (a form of arterial hypertension). Likewise, repeated emotions sustained by purely psychological conflicts will not fail to constitute these states as a chronic case of hypertension or hyperacidity of the gastric acid.

The discussion thus clearly presents that the patient does not singularly depend on the nervous system and the organs, but also on the surrounding environment like the society. Thus, it is not feasible to develop a complete understanding of a patient without knowing their conflicts, family, history, and their environment. This implicitly underlines the influence of social factors on the psychic life.

Relationship between Psychological and Social Facts

In the past, it was widely believed that human nature is immutable, and remains constant throughout history. Correspondingly, the field presented a tendency to analyze every psychological subject as a singular entity in the world. However, presently it has been established that the behavior of an individual presents potential alteration according to the social context. **Therefore, instead of a universal human nature, there exists a multiplicity of human conditions.**

The psychological traits may be widely considered as innate and of an organic origin. However, these are actually modeled by social influences. For example, the psychological differences commonly observed between men and women may not essentially be attributed to the anatomy-physiological distinction of the sexes. The gender-based differences appear very early, in fact, the personalities tests applied in America and in Europe are indicative of heightened emotional awareness amongst girls at a very early age than the boys. However, this distinction might have sourced from their individual education aligned with all sorts of "femininity" and "virility" misconceptions. These influences usually are instilled at very early malleable age of children and correspondingly a diverse education would undoubtedly impact an entirely different psychological effect. The

American ethnologist, Margaret Mead, evidenced this phenomenon in her studies of the Melanesian people. These tribes present a dominant women population who cultivate the land, go fishing, hunting, and deal with trade and government. Conversely, the Melanesian men are docile and fearful, devoted to religious practices and fine arts. It is easy to multiply these examples pertaining to the influence of the society on the human activity, on the intellectual and on the affective life.

The Influence of Society on Human Activities

In addition, habits, as well as the voluntary behaviors, bear the mark of social environments. It has been observed that majority of habits express pattern and tendencies through individual social life, like how to eat, how to swim, and even how to walk. Marcel Mauss, a French sociologist, with expansive academic work traversing the boundaries between sociology and anthropology, calls all of these modes of activity as "the techniques of the bodies." He further adds that these activities assume diverse constructs according to individual education and civilization. Mauss, asserts that there are no natural ways to stand or walk. The Neanderthal man, for example, had arched legs as they normally assume a crouching stance. The will itself, which is defined as the power to resist instincts, is inseparable from the demands of society. Thus, such activities influence the adaptation patterns of the biologically paradoxical behaviors such as voluntary celibacy and voluntary fasting by an individual.

Influence of Society on the Intellectual Life

The very form of thought and its content are impacted by the influences from individual social environment. The individual's thought processes are governed by concept (i.e. by general ideas). Abstract and general ideas are concepts by which we transcend our singular and ineffable experiences and are modes of communication that we can share with other fellow humans. Evidently, there is no thought in language as correspondingly it is from the society where we receive language. Thus, it does not require from the individual any operation of thought but of learning. Similarly, the content of our thoughts also bears the mark of our individual society. There is a possibility that less evolved societies easily form irrational magical practices or absurd superstitions, while it is less common that highly technologically evolved societies where science triumphs tends to give the members of society a better ability to do positive criticisms. Thus, it is certain that our ideas are sourced equally from the epochs of our family, our social class and our environment.

Influence of Society on Affective Life or Feelings

The expression of feelings and the affectivity itself depends upon the cultural environment and likewise the feeling and meaning of love is influenced by its relative era. For instance, the people did not love in the Middle Ages the same way as in the 18th century. In the Greco-Roman antiquity, women were despised and the feeling of love was devalued, while in the Middle Ages, women took on a new value, both under the influence of Christianity and under the influence of Barbarian invasions.

American psychologists of recent times have very precisely studied the relations of affectivity and civilization. For example, the affective maturity depends on social influence; for instance, the age of puberty shows variance with the characteristics of civilization. Correspondingly, the age of puberty was much advanced when the relationships between boys and girls were free. However, these ages presented delay when these relations were paralyzed by taboos. Indeed, the notion of adulthood is a social as well as a physiological fact. For instance, in our civilization, a 15-year-old male is only a child, almost a schoolboy economically dependent on his family. While, in the 17th century, a 15-year-old female was often married and able to become an accomplished housewife, thus considered to be an adult.

American psychoanalysis has accorded an ever-greater place to the sociological considerations. Bronisław Kasper Malinowski, a Polish anthropologist, was often considered one of the most important 20th century anthropologists and Abram Kardiner, an American anthropologist and psychoanalyst, was most famously known for his seminal 1941 study The Traumatic Neuroses of War. Several modern specialists considered Kardiner's research as a key initial work on the psychological trauma. These two re-thought Freudianism in relation to sociological data; (Freudianism will be further elaborated on in Chapter 4). Malinowski in his expansive works evidences the variation of the "super-ego" content with cultures. For example, in studies on Papuans (the natives people of the new British Guinea), Malinovski has shown that the Oedipus complex does not exist in matriarchal societies, were children are raised by their uncle from the mother's side. Similarly, Kardiner studied the interaction between psychic phenomena and social phenomena, stating that if the social institutions accord a shape to the individuals, they take back their strengths and meanings from the psychological needs of individuals.

The functional sociology asserts the same principle and the discussions entailed endeavor to enlighten its principles by sketching as an example, the psycho-sociological analysis of social prejudices.

How can we explain a prejudice – for example, a racial prejudice?

It is a well-known fact that functionalist sociologists sought the function of prejudice, and wondered about the psychological need satisfied by this function. Similarly, life in society often requires individuals to repress their tendencies, as well as their desires and social life, thus provokes in the individual, several kinds of frustrations that trigger aggressiveness. Specifically, such aggressiveness can be deemed dangerous for the group who seeks to protect themselves by providing that individual with "safety covers." This phenomenon can be well exemplified with the anti-Semitism of the Nazis, which shows the isolation of a restricted group that is allowed to be hated and poorly treated by others as a scapegoat. In such cases, prejudice serves as a tool to drain the aggressive forces caused by frustrations and subsequently harbored by us.

The psychosocial interactions are equally essential as the psycho-physiological relationships. However, does this imply that psychology must meld these two disciplines of sociology and physiology or keep them separate to retain specificity? The discipline of psychology thus needs both the physiological and sociological explanations. In psychology, all the elements of the explanation must intersect and present a relationship with the personal history of the subjects with more or less harmonious synthesis behavior of physiological and social determinants.

In the perspective of Daniel Lagache, there is a need for a clinical psychology that considers the concrete individual as a complex and unique whole, in the context of their personal history. This psychology will provide an insight on the conduct of a subject by establishing its senses, structure, genesis, and conflicts. Specifically, this individual perspective will prevent psychology from being confined to the definition of a science in the strict sense of the word. Correspondingly, to understand it, psychology must be viewed as an art, rather than as a science.

"The separation of psychology from the premises of biology is purely artificial, because the human psyche lives in indissoluble union with the body."

Carl Jung

CHAPTER 3:

TENDENCIES AND DESIRES

Mankind is a dynamic being with inclinations, needs, and desires, which are typically referred to as tendencies. A tendency is, by definition, a power of action or a direction underpinned by a specific requirement. A need is a bodily, organic tendency while a desire is a conscious tendency of itself and it is the root of our ego. **Thus, without any desire, there will be no ego.**

Instinct is a tendency, which is satisfied by an innate know-how in the animal. Aristotle has talked about the struggle that has been evidenced between the pleasure and reality principle. He said, "Although desires arise which are opposed to each other, as is the case when reason and appetite are opposed, it happens only in creatures endowed with a sense of time. For reason, on account of the future, bids us resist, while desire regards the present; the momentarily pleasant appears to it as the absolutely pleasant and the absolutely good, because it does not see the future." Desire can, therefore, work against virtue.

Traits that Characterize a Tendency

A tendency is a force, which is oriented towards an object. It is characterized essentially by the elements of tension and finality. It is, in fact, a search for the object. The notion of tendency implies equally the ideas of disposition and virtuality, which, in turn implies the dynamism of a tendency that pre-exists before any experience and that directs thought and behavior. The tendency is a virtual power that wants to be translated into action. Therefore, though it may escape observation because of its virtuality, it reveals itself when it translates as an act.

The Classification of Tendencies

Herein, the book presents four main types of tendencies: (i) tendencies resulting from the need to live, (ii) inner-individual tendencies, (iii) ideal tendencies, and (iv) social tendencies.

1. Tendencies resulting from the need to live:

- Tendencies to eat, drink, and sleep

- Tendencies of sexuality (the search for pleasure, perpetuation of the species, and more)

- Tendencies of mobility (playing sports, walking, dancing, and more)

- Tendencies to exercise one's senses (our need to see and hear, curiosity in its sensitive form in the child, and more)

All of these tendencies are physical in nature and thus reduced to the body. Correspondingly, an excessive satisfaction of these tendencies can lead to "frenzy", thereby necessitating the need to master them with the use of will power.

2. Inner-individual tendencies:

- The tendency to live together in groups and to socialize with fellow humans. This is called "the gregarious instinct" (i.e. the desire to be in contact with others).

- Maternal love

- Affective contagion

3. **Ideal tendencies:**

- Ideal tendencies refer to those tendencies that align themselves to great human values:

- Religious tendency

- Moral tendency (to seek the good)

- Aesthetic tendency (aimed at beauty and art)

- Intellectual tendency (focused on the truth)

4. **Social tendencies:**

- Family tendency

- Professional tendency

- Patriotic tendency

The Problem of the Nature of Tendencies

A tendency implies a disposition and virtuality only revealed through the means of various states of consciousness, affective states, pleasure, pain, and behaviors. This thus begs the question: If the tendency can be defined by affective states and behavior? In order to generate an answer, let us consider the Empiricist and the Behaviorist viewpoints.

The Empiricist Point of View

According to Étienne Bonnot de Condillac, a French empiricist philosopher and epistemologist from the 18th century, the entire philosophy is confined to a play of sensations. Herein significance is allocated to the sensation, which stems from the object itself (i.e. the experience). The conscious subject is in fact, only a passive receptor that receives the projections from external stimulant. For example, as soon as I see a rose, I am compelled to smell it and as I satisfy my instinct, this experience gives me pleasure. This pleasure furthermore creates in me a desire (a tendency) to smell the rose again. Therefore, it can be safely inferred that a tendency does not constitute the primary force in us, and is not innate, but rather acquired.

Condillac denied the very existence of a tendency prior to any experiment and rather he believed that this sensation gives birth to it. For example, the pleasure accompanied with the smell of a rose, is a pleasure memory, which in the absence of the rose inspires the desire to smell it again. This first action is not the tendency but rather it is the memory of pleasure or sensation, which leads to the development of tendency as a consequence.

Undoubtedly, past pleasures orientate an individual' current tendencies and as also exemplified through food tastes, these tendencies are created or shaped by memory. However, these pleasures singularly do not lead to the creation of tendencies.

The preexisting tendency before any experience is a predisposition and thus through experience, it reveals itself, and it becomes conscious of itself – as a desire. "Between tendency and desire there is no difference, however, the desire is the tendency that is conscious of itself," said Baruch Spinoza, a Dutch philosopher who provided the groundwork for the 18th century enlightenment and modern biblical criticism, including modern conceptions of the self and the universe. Moreover, "The tendency is given to us by affectivity. However, it does not define it," said Jules Lachelier, a French philosophy professor.

The Behaviorist Point of View

According to Ribot, mankind is a machine, which combines responses with stimuli. Correspondingly, the repetition of a movement along its intersect and association with objects leads to the creation of tendencies in an individual. Thus, the consequent development of the habit, pertains to a repetition of those acts, which created the tendencies. Thus, if the movement constitutes the tendency, every movement of living beings, consequently refers to a tendency. For example, the student who learns the habit of attending school every day does not have a tendency to go to school on a weekend or a bank holiday.

Specifically, habits do not create a tendency but they do orient it towards a determined object. Thus, the act of smoking corresponds to a taste of tobacco, and the specific taste of tobacco is a particular form, which leads to the creation of the need of this excitant in smokers. Likewise, the taste of alcohol responds to a tonic need for the functioning of the heart of the stomach and the brain.

Moreover, it is incorrect to claim that a habit can increase the strength of a tendency. In fact, a habit does facilitate the execution of the tendency but does not affect the strength of a tendency. For example, the habit of drinking or smoking becomes irresistible because several tendencies of the mind and the body learn to be satisfied through them. Thus, drinking responds to a need of relaxation after fatigue and the need to socialize with others. Therefore, movement and behavior do not define a tendency; the tendency manifests itself via behavior expressed through movement.

Alternatively, although a tendency is expressed by a movement towards an object, all movements are not necessarily a tendency. At this level, Maurice Pradines, a French Philosopher, presented a distinction between "tending at" and "tending toward." For example, on noticing a dangerous zone, an individual usually tends to move away from it. Or, when I feel my hand is going to burn, I tend to remove it. In these cases "tending at" is not a tendency. In such a situation, as I tend to move away from the object, the true tendency is altruistic. Specifically, it consists in tending towards an object or a being, in order to fill a void. "The tendency is a feeling of void in which only an external object can fulfill," said Maurice Pradines.

Thus, the tendency is neither created by experience, nor by habit, in fact this initial predisposition in us forms the basis of our physical dynamism. It escapes direct observation, which only acknowledges and recognizes the affective states and behaviors. Correspondingly, studies evidence that several psychologists, follow the example of Comte, and attempt a rejection of the notion of tendency by comparing it with a sort of metaphysical explanation. However, in alignment with previous experiences, the notion of tendency cannot be ignored without reducing mankind to a machine with reflexes. Thus, despite its metaphysical aspect, the notion of tendency remains indispensable to the understanding of human conduct.

Plasticity of Tendencies

Tendencies are hidden forces, which are as described earlier, directed toward a goal and also referred to as spontaneous impulses. This attribute of a force, accords tendency the specific characteristic of dynamism and therefore it presents a certain margin of plasticity. To call a tendency, elastic means it is neither a fixed point nor an immutable point. Specifically, a tendency is shaped, enriched, and always wears a mask that hides it. As it is said by the American author Christopher Barzak, "Nothing is more real than the masks we make to show each other who we are." Likewise, Albert Burloud, a French psychologist, affirmed, "that the theme of a tendency is transposable and plurivalent," even when the theme remains immutable. Thus, the experience of pleasure or displeasure, habit, and memory enriches the tendencies that are subsequently transformed into new internal dispositions.

Burloud has established at the diverse level of tendencies a distinction between the pattern of a tendency and its corresponding theme. The scheme projects the fundamental and general structure of the tendency while the theme is the particular expression of this tendency. For example, when we eat, eating constitutes the scheme and the object, like an apple, constitutes the theme.

Charles Baudouin, a French-Swiss psychoanalyst, has described the plasticity of tendencies, with the proposition of the distinction between the verb and the object. Wherein, in the 1st case scenario, while the tendency can be placed on another object, the verb remains constant. Like in the example of a hunter who, instead of hunting birds, hunts deer. Similarly, in the 2nd scenario, the tendency can take on a new expression, wherein the verb undergoes a change, with the object remaining constant, as evidenced in love relationships when love turns into hate. Again there is a third case possibility, wherein the tendency can completely modify its expression. The modification concerns the object and the verb. In this case the hunter becomes very old and is unable to hunt, and instead collects books about hunting. These examples clearly indicate that deep examination of the problems in the plasticity of tendencies owes its work to psychoanalysis. In addition, psychoanalysis shows us that tendencies are transformed, subjugated, or repressed.

Specifically, the subjugation is a transformation of a tendency towards spirituality, which also presents a possibility of the transformation of a tendency in the opposite direction. However, the consequently developed aggressiveness of a child to the wandering of the parents can later lead to anxiety or self-punishment. Transfer is a modality of the plasticity of tendencies and it is manifested by contiguity. For example, a lover transfers his/her honest tenderness for his/her other half, towards the objects belonging to this other half. Or the transfer can be by resemblance, as in the case of a lover who sympathizes with all the people who resemble his/her other half.

Correspondingly, the modern psychology aims to study the problem of plasticity in an even more profound way, and explains it within the context of three processes: (i) socialization, (ii) spiritualization, and (iii) individualization. Our tendencies bear the mark of our social life and relatively, the society weighs on us because it is capable of shaping tendencies, and it is society, too, which gives objects to satisfy these tendencies.

Tendencies Can Also be Spiritualized and Intellectualized

Spiritualization is the entry of a tendency in the general aspect of the mind. And refers to nothing but the sublimation of a tendency. A tendency that is spiritualized is an overcoming of banality and mediocrity; and in fact, it is an attachment to our values.

At the end, the tendencies become individualized, which constitutes a psychic fact. Tendency is an element of the wholeness of an individual, and as such each element draws its meaning from this wholeness. Thus, the past of an individual, and his/her intelligence, passion, character, education, and culture contribute to the development of the tendency, as well as to its manifestation and to its orientation there is an individual or personal stamp.

The Problem of Fundamental Desire

This question comprehensively projects the problem of fundamental desire: Can the multiple and complex aspects of our tendencies be reduced to a unity? Are our tendencies all derived from a single original fundamental tendency?

In an attempt to answer these questions, let us consider in a combined fashion, the opinion of the French author Francois De La Rochefoucauld and that of the German philosopher Freidrich Nietzsche. Both the scholars, converge all our tendencies to egoism, and strive to derive the altruist from egoism; and egoism alone is presented hence as a primitive instinct. Altruism, in such a scenario, constitutes a tendency that is manifested in various forms, more or less a disguised of pride, self-love, and everything for oneself. Francois De La Rochefoucauld said, "The refusal of praise is only the wish to be praised twice," and "Pity is often a reflection of our own evils in the ills of others." In the same perspective, Nietzsche adopts a similar point of view: "Mankind," he said, "love only their own inclinations, and not what an individual leans to."

So, originally mankind only has love for the self, for which he/she sacrifices the happiness of others. Hence, the acts of an individual to make others happy, are only oriented towards increasing self-happiness. Then everything comes back to self-love, the only original tendency.

What Values do These Findings Have, From a Psychological Point of View?

First, we must admit that egoism is not natural to mankind, rather it is acquired. In reality, human nature is neither egoistic nor altruistic, and self-love can only be born with the development of self-consciousness. Selfishness is not a primitive tendency, with which we are born, because it presupposes provision and calculation. This, in turn, necessitates an intellectual development and thus it does not constitute a first datum.

Indeed, Rochefoucauld's theory is generally pessimistic and we can oppose through the several instances of spontaneous dedication. Our desires, in essence, are pure and innocent, and in fact, are poisoned with the psychologist's reflection. Correspondingly, the French philosopher Jean-Paul Sartre said, **"I am no longer sure of anything, if I satiate my desires, I sin but I deliver myself from them; if I refuse to satisfy them, they infect the whole soul."**

Furthermore, according to its definition, the tendency is not egoistic because any tendency is centrifugal, (i.e. it uses an external object) and for the same reason, Maurice Pradines said, "All our tendencies are spontaneously altruistic." Relatively, egoism consists of taking as its object not the object of the tendency but the pleasure resulting from the possession of this object. For the egoistic, pleasure is the ultimate goal. The ancient Romans, for example, vomited at the end of a feast to restart the pleasure of eating. One must, therefore, carefully distinguish between an act "for pleasure" and an act done "with pleasure."

But Is the Centrifugal Character of the Tendency Preventing it from Referring to the Subject?

We can safely admit that fundamental tendencies such as dietary and sexual tendencies conform to egoistic tendencies. Therefore, to satisfy them, the individual initially aims specifically to restore a balance of the organism. Correspondingly, Dr. Charles Odier, a Swiss psychoanalyst, tells us that, in addition to bio-psychological tendencies, we have "tendencies-values," which comprise the aims of our values. Similarly, bio-psychological tendencies aim at an object (food or sexual) and on the achievement of satisfaction they become latent. Conversely, the aims of certain values (Like: Selfless or authentic friendship, aesthetic tendency, the search for truth, etc.) are not interrupted by their satisfaction owing to their unquenchable nature. While a purely sexual love hardly survives to its complete satisfaction, also an authentic friendship develops in time and presents longevity while living it, because herein the other is not considered as an object, but as a value.

In an analogous fashion, the aim of tendencies oriented towards beauty and truth cannot be satisfied, because beauty and truth are in fact, not objects but values. The individual who pursues them does not only seek to find a balance by reducing organic tension, but also to always go beyond the self. Thus, these tendencies are said to be altruistic.

La Rochefoucauld's perspective sheds insight on egoistic tendencies that can be disguised as pseudo-values out of the need of improving their satisfaction. Similarly, even though, the love of beauty and truth is not always sincere, it does not imply that beauty and truth do not exist as values. Moreover, La Rochefoucauld states, "Hypocrisy is the homage vice pays to virtue," which seem to imply that he recognized the existence of true values.

The Role of Tendencies
in the Psychic Life

The tendency, which is the power of action or a direction based on our requirements, is an important notion in psychology. It is, indeed, the primordial fact of our psychic life. A tendency is fundamental to our affective, active, and intellectual life. It constitutes the basis of feelings, emotion and passion; the basis of the acquisition of habits and will; as well as the basis for the perception of imagination, attention, and memory.

People are dynamic beings with tendencies, needs, and inclinations, which we generally call tendencies. It has been observed that typically, mankind presents a preference for their own inclinations and not towards what he/she externally leans. Thus, it is apparent that all these tendencies converge back to egoism and also presents the extensive diversity of mankind.

A need is an organic corporeal tendency; a desire is a conscious tendency of itself. Instinct is a tendency that is satisfied by an innate knowledge in the animal. The tendency is virtual, i.e. it is a power that wants to be translated into action.

Does mankind only present love for their inherent inclinations and not actually towards their external inclinations? Alternatively, is mankind always egoistic or altruistic?

Mankind is a spirited being with diverse tendencies or needs like:

social, inter-individual, ideal, and vital order. Correspondingly, Nietzsche affirmed that mankind loves only their inclinations and not toward what they lean.

This discussion raises the question: Up to what measure should we agree with Nietzsche? Aren't our tendencies still altruistic? And don't they seek the object for the object?

Do You Think that a Tendency is an Unavailable Postulate to Psychology?

For an optimal discourse, it is necessary to begin by explaining the meaning of the word postulate. By definition, the postulate is a fundamental and a necessary proposition for the foundation of a geometric system. For example, the whole of Euclidean geometry is based on five postulates known as Euclid's postulates.

The tendency assumes in psychology identical characteristics, which are indispensable despite of its virtuality and offers a scientific explanation for several psychological phenomena. Hence, it is also necessary for the explanation of affectivity and behavior. Therefore, it would be a mistake to derive it from affectivity in the corresponding way as the Empiricists or from behavior in the manner of Behaviorism. It is considered as the reference point in the explanation of the imperative concepts like the will, the habit, the memory, and the perception.

What would be the definition of a tendency, given the definition of the word postulate? Would the tendency be described as indispensable to explain the affectivity and the behavior?

The Empiricist Theory reduced the concept of tendency to affectivity;

however, affectivity rather should be explained by the tendency. In a corresponding manner, the Behaviorists reduced the tendency to behavior and movement. This is indicative of the extensive dependability of several psychological phenomenon on the concept of tendency and as such, psychology cannot do without the tendency. Therefore, indeed, the tendency presents an imperative explanation of all our behavior: habit, will, memory, perception, emotion, passion, and more.

CHAPTER 4:

CONSCIOUSNESS AND SUBCONSCIOUSNESS

The French philosopher André Lalande said, **"that consciousness is the intuition that the mind possesses of its states and its actions;"** similar to the states of mind where we recognize and re-recognize ourselves, i.e. we are in constant awareness of our social identity, our name, nationality, birth place, etc. In other words, it is the domain of our will, of our gestures and thoughts, of which we assume full responsibility.

Levels of Consciousness

Consciousness does not project a complete cover to the totality of the psyche. It knows and undergoes degrees of variations in intensity or luminosity because it is active, fluid, and changeable.

In babies: In the maternal womb, the child has been observed to perform various movements, but these are subconscious movements.

In newborns: Infants do not see nor hear yet and are enclosed in a world of their own. They present their reactions by exhibiting their needs of hunger, thirst, and other basic wants. Gradually, their sensitivity evolves and with the help of their senses, they begin to gain awareness of the unity of their body, but not yet of the external world. At this stage, their consciousness is still egocentric (ego = centrist, I = center) and it is only later on that they begin to distinguish between the world and its objects. This is followed by the "animist" stage (they start giving a soul to things), where the children start to animate everything they see. Subsequent to this is the "artificiality" stage, where they perceive the prefabricated world. Clearly, children take time to really become aware of themselves and their personality.

<u>In adults:</u> Here we can distinguish several levels of consciousness, ranging from the highest to the lowest (or simplest) as following:

- The supra-consciousness, which translates to the peak of consciousness: It is the activity of invention and creation.

- Thoughtful consciousness, or awareness (I know that I know): This level presupposes a doubling of the self. It starts by a return to oneself so as to allow the subject to analyze their feelings and actions, then to judge them and to go back to the reason of their underlying cause. This consciousness is composed of 3 moments of separation:

1. It separates me from the world. René Descartes, a French philosopher, mathematician, and scientist, elaborated on this with the example of his own doubt, "If I doubt it is that I think and if I think it is that I am."

2. It separates me from myself. Reflective consciousness implies a distinction between the subject and the object between a self that knows and a self to know. I can know myself only by doubling myself (me = observer, and I = observed). As the French

philosopher Emile-Auguste Chartier, also known as Alain said, "Consciousness presupposes a separation of the self from the self."

3. It separates me from others. I know of others only by their gestures and their words, and their conscience actually escapes me.

• Spontaneous consciousness, which is a direct and confused consciousness of what is happening inside us and outside of us. For example, I am sad and, therefore, I suffer. I have a good or bad temper. It actually refers to a primitive consciousness that informs me of my immediate state. Correspondingly, this consciousness does not present longevity because it is limited to what I think about my suffering. This conscience is thus no longer immediate and becomes reflective.

• Passive consciousness is observed when awakening or during surgical anesthesia, where the patient passes through different stages of consciousness before plunging into the darkness of the subconscious. This state has been in majority of instances experienced by people who have been put to sleep medically.

The Different Understandings of Consciousness

The least favorable understandings:

The popular conception compares consciousness with a light that illuminates, as in the instance of awareness or attention to certain parts of the consciousness in our social field and horizons.

The Behaviourist understandings (some people that adhered to it are Ribot, Watson, Condillac, Hume, etc.). According to these scholars, consciousness is an epiphenomenon, a phenomenon to be added and individually, consciousness is incapable of exercising any action.

The most favorable understandings:

The classical findings from Descartes, that states that the soul is a substance whose essence is thought, which means intuition and an immediate knowing.

Phenomenologists (some people who adhered to it are Edmund Husserl, Jean-Paul Sartre, and Maurice Merleau-Ponty). According to these scholars, all consciousness is essentially "intentionality" because all consciousness is consciousness of something, implying that it aims at an object. For them consciousness is directed to a world that it does not possess; however towards which it never ceases to point itself. For example, perception, memory, love, and hatred are not internal states, but ways aimed at the external world.

Modern Psychology (some people who adhered to it are William James, Bergson, Pierre Janet, etc.). Pierre Janet, a pioneering French psychologist, philosopher and psychotherapist, said that consciousness is not only a light that illuminates but also one that modifies, which is a reaction. For example, the consciousness of success is a conduct of triumph, which in fact, adds to the action of success. For Maurice Pradines, consciousness is a gathering of knowledge and know-how, an activity of synthesis, mental availability, adaptation, and understanding.

The Nature of Consciousness

Consciousness is an action, a pure dynamism of the subject that is projected towards the external world. Correspondingly, Edmund Husserl, a German philosopher, claimed that consciousness is intentionality. It is a way to target the world and not a thing or an inner life. **"All consciousness is consciousness of something,"** it's always a goal or a direction toward something outside of me.

When I see pots of flowers on my balcony, this perception is not an internal state. It is an act of my consciousness, which is aimed at an object of the external world. Correspondingly, if I remember a day of my vacation, remembering is not a purely internal reality; it is an act by which my consciousness is directed towards a certain event in my past. This presents a coordinative image as that of emotion and feelings. For example, when a man rushes towards me and I feel fear, here, again, my fear appears not as inner information but as an attitude towards an external stimulus. This is indicative of directing my consciousness to an external reality of the world, because the most intimate and the most subjective world of feelings, does not escape this law that "all consciousness is consciousness of something." A feeling is, for me, a way of being in the world. To love and to hate are ways of directing myself towards others.

Consciousness is a function of discernment. It seeks to recognize and identify the elements of a particular situation. For example, in relation to a dissertation topic, I try to understand the words, the sentences, and the questions relevant to the topic

Consciousness is also an activity of selection and organization. The word selection, by default implies the presence of a choice. Correspondingly, from the objects presented to it, consciousness privileges certain objects and remains insensitive to others. It was Bergson who developed with the most conviction the idea that all consciousness means choice. He showed that all consciousness shows an intersect with the present, the real, and the action. For instance, my current task solicits my consciousness and correspondingly, I evoke, for example, all the memories that are useful to me to accomplish what I am doing in the present moment.

In the same way consciousness is memory, a person could never be conscious if he/she did forget the teachings or experiences they received in the past. To be conscious is to react to the present with all its past experiences, towards responding in an improved manner to the world. Consciousness is not only memory; it is the function of anticipating, because humans are the beings of the past. Mankind is the only being who perceives the problems of the future. This is because, humans project and the consciousness appears as a telescope towards the future, which allows us to predict events before they happen.

In addition, Janet said that consciousness is a power of synthesis. It is an activity of coordination and control. In a state of perfect psychic health, consciousness plays the role of "cum-scientia," which means of synthesis accompanied by knowing. The synthetic power of consciousness is large enough to envelop an individual's various activities. For example, if I write a paper of answers to questions that I am being asked, here I am aware of my actions and I control my own thoughts.

Consciousness is also metaphysics of the self, it is at the root of each will because it is the "I think" and at the same time "I want."

Similarly, consciousness is an instrument of freedom. When I am conscious of a situation, I possess and dominate it.

Finally, for consciousness to arise, it requires a double condition: First, the presence of a vital problem necessitating an adaptation response and then, second, a particular difficulty, which requires a choice. Consciousness arises when spontaneous activity meets failure, and consciousness becomes all the more intense when the situation is perilous.

We conclude with Bergson that, "consciousness is a link between what has been and what will be. It is a bridge between the past and the future." Georg Wilhelm Friedrich Hegel, a German philosopher, said, "what elevates mankind in relation to the animal, is the consciousness of being an animal… Because mankind knows that we are an animal, therefore we cease to be one." Furthermore, becoming consciously self-aware is not a comfortable process, as it requires constant work. It does not feel good to acknowledge or recognize things about ourselves that are hidden in the subconscious, nor does it feel good to recognize truths that we don't want to be true.

The Nature of the Subconscious or Unconscious

The everyday use of this term "unconscious" refers to individuals under anesthesia or with a mental condition, which means they are without consciousness. However, in the physiological sense, we use this term "subconscious" to describe the states and acts that escape consciousness even though they are present in an ordinary person. Examples include, movements of blood circulation, hair growth, fingernail growth, etc.

In the psychological sense, there are two aspects of the subconscious:

1. The innate subconscious: The simple reflexes.

2. The acquired subconscious: The habit.

The Pathological Subconscious

This refers to all that what is not explicitly conscious in the psychic life, meaning that which remains subconscious to the person and he/she has no consciousness of them. Moreover, it constitutes the part of the latent psyche, which is made up of psychological and dynamic desires and processes, such as the tendencies that we could not dispose of that have been repressed (because they have escaped our consciousness but which nevertheless manage to be manifested in certain acts of the daily life). Examples include dreams, forgetting, lapses in memory, etc.

Refusal of the Psychic Subconscious

For Théodule-Armand Ribot and the psychology of the 1st person, all that is psychic is conscious and all that is subconscious is physiological.

For René Descartes, because consciousness and psychic life are coextensive, it would be contradictory to speak of a subconscious psychic life.

For modern phenomenologists (Jean-Paul Sartre, Edmund Husserl) the only way for consciousness to exist is to know that it exists. "All consciousness is consciousness of something."

Emile-Auguste Chartier, considered that it is a folly to speak of the subconscious because, for him, "knowing is knowing that we know." Therefore, we have awareness of things.

For Jean-Paul Sartre, mankind is a being in a situation - surroundings.

Acceptance of the Psychic Subconscious

For Gottfried Leibniz, German polymath and philosopher, the subconscious is only a degradation of consciousness, the product of a regression or a decrease in the consciousness.

For Pierre Janet, the subconscious is a drop in mental synthesis.

For Bergson, the subconscious is not what is not conscious, but it refers to what does not currently appear in the psyche. The subconscious exists but it is latent, virtual, and inactive, which explains the preservation of memories.

It is noteworthy that the notions of a psychic subconscious are only possible within the framework of psychology, when reviewed and studied in the third person. Because psychology is considered to be the science of behavior, a behavior that is or becomes subconscious does not cease to be a psychic fact.

For Sigmund Freud, the subconscious is the psychic region of the "id," where it originates and develops the first impulses and whose libido is the nucleus. This is the domain where the repressed tendencies remain and are condemned to be censored, rejected outside of the consciousness, and consequently ignored by the person.

This subconscious is hidden, but it constitutes a reservoir of explosive charges that sprout and manifest themselves as warnings, particularly in dreams. Freud said that the conscious life "Would be comparable to a book of which only a few pages survive, the others having been lost. What is lacking is necessary for understanding what remains." Accordant to this, our conscious life exists in continuity with our subconscious life. As such, one can understand the real psychological life only by relying on the first as much on the second because the consciousness and the subconscious are in a constant exchange.

The Psychoanalytic Method

Before discovering his psychoanalytic method, Freud practiced hypnosis, with the aim to make conscious that what is subconscious. However, Freud considered hypnosis to be an inhuman method, i.e. brutal on the free will of mankind. Consequently, the pathogenic processes did not disappear definitively and concurrently the morbid symptoms soon reappeared. For these reasons, he thought of a more humane and more effective method: psychoanalysis. Psychoanalysis is a method of deep psychological research at the service of the subconscious and is also used as a therapeutic method to treat mental disorders.

Following the observation of his patients, Freud managed to make four discoveries, which progressively helped him with the development of the psychoanalytic method:

1. He discovered the existence of mental illnesses.

2. He identified psychic trauma to underpin these mental illnesses.

3. He identified the subconscious nature of this trauma.

4. He also revealed that when the subconscious becomes conscious, it ceases to be harmful.

The psychoanalytic method consists of transforming the subconscious state into a conscious state. The psychoanalyst analyzes the subconscious from the relevant manifesting behaviors:

- The automatic association of ideas according to the rule of non-omission.

- The missed acts, like the lapses, forgetfulness, etc.

- The dream, which is indicative of the disguised realization of a repressed desire.

- Neuroses and psychoses.

Therapeutics is based on the relation of the therapist and the patient; the clinical neurosis substitutes for a therapeutic neurosis or a neurosis of transfer.

The unfolding of the psychoanalytic method (latent, patent, apparent, and premonitory):

The psychiatrist invites the patient to lie on a couch. Then the psychiatrist sits behind him/her in silence. The patient then enters an almost dreamy state, which is induced by the psychiatrist. He/she does not seem to hear and the psychiatrist only rarely interrogates the patient. This thus creates a setting wherein the patient feels at home. The only rule that the patient must respect is the non-omission (i.e. not to hide anything), and the patient must say everything even if it is disagreeable. From time to time, the psychiatrist may judge it useful to halt the patient in his/her discourse to propose the last word as an inducer, to help the patient to project some free association from this word.

The hidden force – the subconscious – prevents the subconscious theme from returning to consciousness due to the expression of silence and hesitation, which Freud calls the resistance. The patient resists his/her own effort to recover the subconscious psychological themes, and this resistance manifests itself in repression. The sagacity of the psychiatrist is in discovering the sensitive points around which this resistance manifests itself.

At a specific time, as deemed appropriate by the psychiatrist, he/she communicates the interpretations to the patient, which would represent the causes of his/her illness. With this revelation, the patient experiences a particular emotional reaction towards the doctor. With this stimulus, he/she subconsciously reproduces the old disorders that caused this illness. It is then said that the patient lives a recovery to transfer what is subconscious to consciousness and this transfer can be positive as much as it can be negative, i.e. that the patient repeats to the psychoanalyst subconscious friendly (positive) or hostile (negative) attitudes.

The imperative role of the psychoanalyst, herein, is to control the transfer (i.e. to bring the patient to consciousness), to recognize this subconscious problem. No healing would take place without this transfer.

The Manifestations of the Subconscious

Subconscious activity is revealed in eight varied ways:

1. **In the psychoanalytic method:** Which happen through transfer or recovery, as explained above.

2. **In the dream:**

Before Freud, we accorded the concept of dreams a metaphysical explanation. The dream was perceived as a communication from a force with the supernatural powers, giving us a kind of a sign that comes from the beyond or a warning that we must decipher. The physiologists have asserted the following physiological explanation of the dream: when the consciousness ceases to be vigilant, the mental images contained in the nerve cells are linked in a random order. However, this explanation is not sufficient and is limited in scope.

Freud gives dreams a psychological sense. Of the dream, he says, "It is fulfillment or satisfaction, in a symbolic way a desire pushed back. Or in a different way it is the royal passage of the subconscious." For Freud, my dreams concern me, reveal me, and present a human meaning. The dream has a meaning in a general way: they express a desire. The first is the desire to continue to sleep. Freud said that the dream is "the guardian of sleep." If, during sleep, for example, I am very thirsty, I will eventually wake up and I will drink, but if I would probably dream that I drank, this fictitious satisfaction will prolong my sleep.

The importance of the nocturnal dream for the exploration of the subconscious lies in the fact that subconscious desires, when repressed in the waking state, are satisfied in dreams. In fact, censorship (constituted by the concern for conveniences and moral ideas), which escapes these forbidden desires in the waking state, is evident in the state of weakened sleep. Thus, the forbidden desires are satisfied in the dream in a determined way, similar to a symbolic veil.

For better comprehension, let us consider an example, borrowed from the American psychoanalyst and psychiatrist Horace Frink. A female patient tells that she dreamed she was in a department store and bought a very expensive, beautiful black hat. The analysis of this dream revealed that the patient was in love with a rich and beautiful young man. Even though she was married and her husband, an elderly man, was suffering from illness. However, the analysis of this dream revealed the subconscious and guilty desires of the patient that were put into action and are symbolically dramatized: the beautiful hat signifies a need of adornment to reduce the fading existence of the man she loves, the costly expense of the hat revealed the desire for wealth, and because the hat was black, mourning is signified, meaning that the woman had a desire to be delivered from her sick husband.

The analysis of the dream allowed Freud to distinguish between two types of content: (i) the patent or manifested content and (ii) the latent content that is hidden. In the dream of the woman with the black hat, the story told constitutes the manifest content, while the explanation given by the psychoanalyst about the images of the dream that translated a subconscious desire constitutes the latent content.

3. In the missing acts (affective deficiency):

- The lapses, refers to errors committed by speaking and writing, which consist of replacing one word by another (without intending to). For example, "I declare the sitting closed," said the President of the Chamber at the beginning of the sitting. "Oh, sorry. I mean open."

- Forgetfulness and clumsiness of all kinds, such as when someone unintentionally loses or misplaces an object that displeases him/her, or forgets a certain appointment. These involuntary acts cannot be explained simply by the awkwardness or weakness of the memory. Moreover, these acts are indicative of a meaning that hides our true and deepest desires.

4. In the psychic diseases of neuroses and psychoses:

These mental disorders result from a conflict between the "id" and the "super-ego." All of the patients with illnesses such as phobias, obsessions, hysteria, and schizophrenia assume an oppressive subconscious desire. Psychologists believe that the gestures of these patients offer an undeniable proof of the existence of the subconscious.

5. In the activity: Indeed, we carry within ourselves a whole background of instincts, tendencies, habits, and hereditary powers, which present roots in the subconscious (as much as the collective subconscious) that originates from society.

6. In affectivity: Affectivity is the part of us of which we are the most unaware. In fact, we do not always know the source of our sympathies and antipathies. Our feelings and passions undergo a

subconscious elaboration, the perception of which is apparent to the thinking consciousness only afterwards. Thus, one is incapable of explaining love at first sight, or some tics like nail biting, lip licking, sniffing, thumb sucking, etc. All these tics appear after the person was emotional and disappear with ease and relaxation.

7. **In imagination and the fabulous universes that it invents:** The subconscious plays a great role in the work of the imagination. Indeed, novelists and artists have sufficiently emphasized the role of the subconscious in their creations.

8. **In perceptions:** What we perceive is interpreted often by our subconscious. For example, different people perceive the same landscape differently. This diversity of meanings and signs for the same landscape finds its origin in our differentially conditioned subconscious.

Irrespective of the expansive previous discussion, it is best to refrain from explaining everything by the subconscious. Correspondingly, it is also necessary to avoid using the subconscious like a stopgap mechanism in absence of availability of explanations for certain states.

What are the Contributions of Psychoanalysis to Psychology? The Psychic Apparatus

The structure of the psychic apparatus was defined by Sigmund Freud and explained in 1927 to constitute of three parts: the id, the ego, and the super-ego. Freud "ascribed the characteristics of being extended in space and of being made up of several portions [id, ego, super-ego]." (*An Outline of Psychoanalysis*, 1940)

According to the online etymology dictionary, the ego is a term in metaphysics that means "the self; that which feels, acts, or thinks," from the Latin word "I," cognate with Old English "ic." ("Ic" was reduced to "I" by the mid-12th-century in northern England, and later everywhere. By the mid-13th-century, it was capitalized as a distinct word).

Sigmund Freud distinguished in the ego what is referred to in Aramaic and Hebrew as "ha-satan," our personal adversary.

The Hebrew word "ha-satan" or "satan" (שָׂטָן) translates to "adversary" and comes from a Hebrew verb meaning "to oppose, to obstruct, or to deceive," and "to cause one to be misled or go astray." Contradictory to popular belief, the first original five books of the Bible rarely used that word. Israel's prophets also hardly ever employed the expression "satan." It gradually crept into Jewish literature during the exile and post-exilic period of Israel's history.

Therefore, who is our adversary in life more than ourselves (our ego-self) with all the negative voices we all hear in our heads. These negative voices invariably invade our thoughts with negativity and fears for the sole purpose to challenge us. **Thus, no one but we are our biggest adversary!**

The Three Parts of the Ego

The id: This is the seat of our basic needs that consists of impulses, instincts, and aggressive sexual and repressed tendencies. It is the engine of our personality structure that includes our unevolved, instinctive part of our brain. It is the place where our basic needs reside. It is based on the pleasure principle and progressively thrives to obtain it with one of its primary functions to avoid pain or displeasure.

The ego: This is the zone of consciousness. It has voluntary and intellectual perceptual activity. The ego acts for the defense of the person, ensuring their adjustment or adaptation with the entourage, to thereby offer the solution of conflicts with reality. Therefore, the ego is subject to the principle of reality and is the driver of the vehicle. It contains the ingredients of our personality that address dealing with reality, and which venture to mediate between the id and super-ego in its relation to the id. Like the id, the ego seeks pleasure and avoids pain at any price. However, unlike the id, the ego is involved with conceiving a realistic strategy to obtain pleasure.

The super-ego: This is the set of moral, social, and religious rules that have been transmitted to us through parental education and social influences. The super-ego imposes the barriers of morality to the impulses coming from the id. Between consciousness and subconsciousness lies the censorship that controls and represses suspicious energies – those that are refused by the super-ego. This activity of censorship is repression. Tendencies that are repressed in the subconscious do not remain inactive and associate with each other to form complexes.

Freud was the first to discuss repression. He described it as our defense mechanism, which arguably it is the most important one. **The process of repression is a subconscious mechanism employed by our ego as a defense method to obstruct our thoughts from becoming conscious.** All thoughts, emotions, feelings, tendencies, and desires that are often repressed are those, which generate in us feelings of guilt originating from the super-ego. For example, in the Oedipus complex discussed in Chapter 2, aggressive thoughts about the same sex parents are repressed.

Therefore, the super-ego is in fact, the driver's assistant, which is responsible for criticism and moralizing. It is that moral part of the personality that we have learned from our environment, parents, social rules, and morals of society. The super-ego's function is to control the id's impulses (such as social prohibitions, aggression taboos, and deviant sexual urges).

Even though the ego and the super-ego may, upon occasion, reach similar decisions, the ego's decision is based on the consequences and the perceived approval or disapproval of the society, while the super-ego's reasons for that decision will be more based on our moral values.

Freud believed that, as babies, all our behaviour is ruled by the id, as this is the focal point of the location of our basic survival instincts, and correspondingly our desires for pleasure-seeking stem from it. With time, as we get older, our ego develops and is shaped basically by environmental influences.

With the progression of time, our concept of the ego has metamorphosed since Freud's explanation. When, in our common language, we describe an individual as having a big ego, we are referring to their self-interest. Though, according to Freud's theory, the more accurate description is to say that they have a "big id." Similarly, when we say that someone is being egotistical, we refer to his/her self-esteem. However, to be loyal to Freud's definition, it simply means we are referring to the conscious part of his/her brain.

Aristotle, who was born in a small Greek colony in Thrace called Stagira in 384-322 BC, discussed the struggle of the id and ego: "There are two powers in the soul which appear to be moving forces – desire and reason. But desire prompts actions in violation of reason... desire... may be wrong." Thus, according to him, it is in fact, the id that directs and controls the adaptation of the subject to the environment. **There is psychic equilibrium when the ego manages to satisfy the requirements of the id, without disturbing the super-**

ego and giving careful cogitation for each reality situation. Consequently, failure of the ego to act normally leads to the development of the psychic troubles.

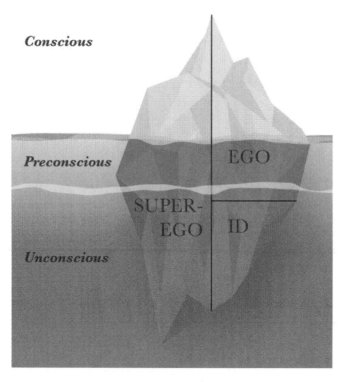

Conscious

Preconscious

EGO

SUPER-
EGO

ID

Unconscious

#1 : FREUD'S ICEBERG METAPHOR OF THE HUMAN PSYCHE

Characteristics of the Ego

The ego constitutes the main component of the development of our personality, with the most primary function of controlling our consciousness and helping us identify what is real in our life. As children, we start to develop individual egos by the ages of two or three, in order to advance the sense of our thoughts, our environment, and the world around us.

According to Freud, we experience three levels of consciousness, were the points of the ego exist in all these levels and constitute the main component of our awareness:

1. Subconsciousness, which is everything outside of our awareness.

2. Pre-consciousness, which is the knowledge and memories that we can retrieve.

3. Consciousness, which is our current awareness.

The ego is subjected to the control of what is called the reality principle (as aforementioned), where all the desires of our id strive to be satisfied in a realistic and socially approved manner. Thus, this reality principle stimulates the ego to consider the pros and cons of a desire, prior to deciding on how to act on it. The ego function is thus to accomplish and achieve those desires in acceptable ways.

Role of Childhood in the Formation of Personality

Psychoanalysis attributes a primordial importance to individual history and especially to the primary relations between the child and their parents. In the words of William Wordsworth, a major English Romantic poet, "the child is the father of man," which is to say that the events of childhood present a significant decisive impact on the formation of the adult personality. The psychological trauma of childhood, and the primary relations of the child and his/her parents are essential pieces of data that hence must be discovered, to emerge from the subconscious so to understand the reactions of an adult subject.

The notion of meaning is also important. All psychic phenomena have a hidden meaning, which can be revealed through psychoanalysis. For example, American psychoanalyst and physician Horace Frink was quoted by French philosopher Roland Dalbiez as being obsessed with insignificant objects, such as a hat and a checkbook. Frink was a founding member of the New York Psychoanalytic Society and the author of one of the first American books on psychoanalysis, but he also suffered from a mental condition that worsened over time, ultimately causing him to be institutionalized. Frink was also one of Sigmund Freud's patients, and stated, "I am going crazy." His obsession with the hat and the checkbook, although strange, is indicative of a very strong meaning because the hat had a red lining and the checkbook was red. It was found that, when the subject was a child, he had wounded his brother involuntarily, causing blood to flow out of the wound. The subject (Frink) experienced a terrible feeling of guilt and he also had repressed this painful memory. The obsession of bloodshed then reappears in symbolic form as an obsession with the color red.

Correspondingly, it has been observed that the most bizarre and hysterical manifestations present a specific meaning, which reveals itself in analysis. For example, an anorexic patient, without presenting any lesion of the digestive tract with absence of any appetite, manifested this conflict obscurely through a sort of subconscious strike of hunger.

So, in the perspective of Freud, instincts, passions, nocturnal dreams, symptoms, and even seemingly absurd neuroses have hidden meanings that are indeed discoverable.

The Importance of Sexuality

The sexual drive or the libido as designated by Freud refers to the search of sensual pleasure in general. Freud speaks of an evolution of sexuality in several stages or phases where the libido gets transfixed on different objects and is identified through these objects.

Sexual impulses, according to Freud, pass through six different stages:

1st – The oral stage: Up to 6 months old. The focus is the mouth and the action of sucking that is dominant in all the infants. All the sensations are judged by the sense of the mouth.

2nd – The late oral stage: From 6-12 months old. The infant tends not move on from sucking to bite, to take, and to keep. This duration presents the first conflict with their environments.

3rd – The anal stage: Between 1 and 3 years old. During this duration, children are potty-trained and this stage presents an increase in the libido, as it is now focused on the anus. In this stage children learn about the cleanliness and control of the sphincter. The child is completely aware at this stage of the fact that he/she is an individual in his/her own right.

4th – The phallic stage: Between 3 and 5 years old. The libido attaches to the genital organs, and the attachment to the parents is subdivided into a libidinal component. This stage is marked by the appearance of the complex – of Oedipus, which consists of the fact that the boy child intensifies his love for the mother. He feels a conflict between his love for his father, whom he now considers a competing rival for the mother's love. The attitude of the girl child is identical, but it is necessary to reverse the terms. The psychic balance of the child is established with progress of time when the boy accepts the father as his father and himself as his son. The same applies to the girl child.

5th – The latency stage: Between 6 years old and the onset of puberty. This stage is characterized by a decrease in sexual drive, as the libido is dormant. It has been observed that the children develop a defense mechanism against their impulses, which are determined by their culture. The child here evidenced to be generally quiet and calm, with virtually no problems or conflicts. There is no aggression or rivalry, as the sexes (fatherly - motherly figure) are elucidated in their mind during this phase.

6th – The genital stage: From puberty to adulthood. After puberty, the attraction of the other sex is manifested in the boy and the girl. This stage marks the beginning of the child's conflicts with the parents, oneself, and with others. It is the most difficult and challenging phase, which if properly implemented, can effect a normal evolution. However, if personal fragility conjoins unfavorable circumstances, for example, excessive maternally inclined education for the boy or excessive paternally inclined education for the girl; then there exists a possibility of regressions to earlier stages, for example, infantilism or probable sexual perversion.

Psychoanalysis after Freud's Discoveries

Alfred Adler, an Austrian medical doctor and psychotherapist, in his work, placed importance on the **Inferiority Complex** and the **Superiority Complex**. His work focused less on sexuality (as compared to Freud) and more on the need to assert oneself and become dominant. He asserted that the essential spring of human activity is not the libido or the will to enjoy, but the will oriented towards power and assertiveness.

It has been observed that the cause of a neurosis is usually a sexual complex or difficulty, or a feeling of inferiority, especially the physical type of inferiority. Correspondingly, the neurotic symptoms constitute a symbolic way of compensating for this inferiority. Therefore, the subconscious processes employed by the ego and are interpreted by Freud through repression have been explained by Adler through the inferiority complex with the use of compensation.

Correspondingly, Carl Jung, a Swiss psychiatrist and psychoanalyst, ensured that both perspectives of explanation of Freud and Adler are equally legitimate. However, he also asserted that the will to enjoyment and the will to power are in fact two distinct manifestations of the same vital energy, which reveal two diverse temperaments. Whereas in Freud's perspective, an individual remains insignificant due to being confined as a source of an aspiration, with a blind thirst to pleasure and a theater of anguish.

Adler, on the other hand, emphasizes the subject that seeks to be safe and to dominate objects and things. These two explanations correspond according to Jung with two different types of characters, i.e. the extrovert and the introvert.

The extrovert is the person who attaches himself or herself explicitly to the object than to the self. In this case the person is looking outwards, is sociable, and is expressive. He or she shows a consistent attempt to adapt to a concrete situation. However, their destiny actually is dependent on the objects found in his/her path. The extrovert belongs to Freudian psychoanalysis.

The introvert is reserved, meditative, easily hesitant, and isolated. To him or her applies the Adlerian concepts.

Notably, one should not believe that the passage from one to the other state of character is impossible. There exists a possibility that the person of action (the extrovert) aspires for contemplation, while the dreamer (the introvert) turns to the inner world, harboring the nostalgia of possible adventures.

The Collective Subconscious According to Jung

Jung distinguishes between the personal subconscious as individual forms of repressed elements, and the collective subconscious as a common heritage for the entire human race and creator of images transmitted discreditably, which are called types. Our subconscious bears the traces not only of the conflicts experienced in our individual childhoods, but also of the most distant anxiety of humanity, which lies at the heart of its history.

Methods of Explanation of the Subconscious

The revolutionary contribution of psychoanalysis is incontestable. Psychoanalysis has completely transformed our current knowledge of mankind. **It revealed to us the narrowness of the field of consciousness and has progressively illuminated a new instinctive and irrational foundation that dominates us in a way which is much more powerful than our reason.** The uncovering of this obscure zone − the subconscious, was one of the greatest discoveries in regards to the human psyche.

The invention of the psychoanalysis method cannot be attributed a lesser significance compared to the descriptive psychology methods. On the contrary, psychoanalysis aims at a more imperative goal of a therapeutic nature. It is unnecessary to repeat what has already been said about Freud's several other great discoveries, because these great discoveries end up imposing themselves on their own.

However, intent to make psychoanalysis an excellent method of exploring the subconscious, Freud found it necessary to widen his door to an extent, which resulted in this method to transform into a systematic philosophy. Here, in the process, Freud committed major errors, as he sought to explain all human behavior and all manifestations of human culture from the pathogenic subconscious.

On the level of a psychic life in general, Freud perceived only instincts and tendencies, which have undergone an impoverishing schematization. Therefore, he reduced all tendencies to only two: sexuality and aggressiveness. In fact, in several ways these two tendencies, on repression, constitute the root of most complexes within the human psyche.

However, Freud was keen on providing an explanation of all human values from the subconscious. Therefore, art has been perceived majorly as the product of a complex, which is the inferiority complex. On this subject, Dr. Jean Delay, a psychiatrist, neurologist and a French writer, said, "Psychoanalysis will only explain to art what has been less artistic." We can add what Roland Dalbiez, the French philosopher best known for his Psychoanalytic Method and the Doctrine of Freud, who correspondingly said, **"Psychoanalysis will not explain to mankind what is less human in him."**

In terms of morality, confusing the moral conscience with the super-ego has been evidenced to be very dangerous, since the moral conscience of a balanced and independent adult is irreducible to the super-ego (it is irreducible to a set of orders and categorical imperatives).

Freud, subsequently progressed to explain religion as an aspect of society, which deeply influences the subconscious, and stated that religions are, but a human creation. In his explanation of it, he confounded the temporal and the spiritual, the profane and the sacred. It is described as a phenomenon of projection; the conduit of a paternal complex. Correspondingly, it is argued that the primitive people projected in the sky the image of a severe and correct earthly father, analogous to the image of a father desired by a child during childhood.

From all what we have discussed, we can affirm that Freudianism is Materialism. Materialism, according to Auguste Comte, is "the explanation of the superior by the inferior." In fact, Freud is a materialist attributed to his attempt towards explaining all the psychic life and all the manifestations of human culture by the inferiority: libido, repressions, and complexes. Thus, psychoanalysis fails to be a science of mankind. **It is simply a science of the subconscious.**

CHAPTER 5 :

<u>EMOTION</u>

Examples of emotions are fear, anger, anguish, shame, joy, sadness, shyness, and more.

An emotion is a momentary and rather violent affective disorder that concerns both the consciousness and the body and is usually caused by a perception or an idea. It presents a winning attribute when it violates the organism and its whole psyche, and it always comprises invasive properties. Emotions are real crises of short duration, as opposed to feelings, which are longer lasting and less intense emotional states. This correspondingly underpins the reason why we oppose emotional-shock to emotional-feeling.

I-The emotion is accompanied by disorders and they are as follows:

1st – Organic: Almost the same in all emotions

2nd – Circulatory: Pallor, redness, and heartbeat

3rd – Respiratory: Gasping and sometimes choking

4th – Muscle: Tremor and nervous laughter

5th – Visceral: Intestinal

6th – Glandular: Tears and sweat

All these disorders present common characteristics of being agitated, i.e. organic disorders that are not adaptive and do not serve any functional purpose.

II-Motor reactions: Cries, sobs, and violent gestures.

III-Mental changes: Lapses of ideas, and the inability to think or judge or to make a decision.

The organic disorders of emotion are directly dependent on both the sympathetic nervous system, which prepares the body for physical and mental activity, and the parasympathetic nervous system, which is responsible for our bodily functions when the individual is at rest. Correspondingly, the center of emotion is a portion of the brain called the hypothalamus. This hypothalamic zone is under the direct dependence of the cerebral cortex that controls and inhibits emotional manifestations. Evidently, even a decerebrated animal continues to experience emotion, as it still possesses the hypothalamus.

The Different Perspectives on the Nature and Mechanism of Emotions

The physiological perspective of James and Lange: The James-Lange Theory

Both, William James, an American philosopher and psychologist, and Carl Lange, a Danish physician who made contributions to the fields of neurology, psychiatry, and psychology, held the view that emotions result from the awareness of the peripheral organic reactions. This clearly implies the generation of an awareness about my emotions via my body organs reactions. Literature review shows that this theory attaches particular importance to peripheral organic disorders as opposed to disorders of the superior nerve center.

Therefore, this theory is opposed to the intellectualist theory and to the opinion of common sense by the modification of the order of succession of these phenomena:

1st Emotional Representation → I see a bear

2nd Emotion → I feel scared

3rd Organic Disorder → I start to tremble

For the physiological theory of James-Lange, we must reverse the order of the last two phenomena. Therefore, the process results the following succession:

1st Emotional Representation → I see a bear

2nd Organic Disorder → I start to tremble

3rd Emotion → I feel scared

Concurrent to James-Lange, we subsequently identify that the notion of a disembodied emotion does not exist. The emotional person has a body, but the organic expression is essentially connected with the central organic conditions, which conform to the hypothalamic centers that depend directly on the cerebral cortex. Similarly, it has been evidenced that a decerebrated animal continues to experience emotions of fear and anger, even though it no longer receives any impression from the periphery of the body. Similarly, one can inject adrenaline into a subject, causing him or her organic troubles without provoking in them the emotion itself. Therefore, clearly a balanced vital state is essential for the conditions of the body to support the psychic conditions, and vice versa.

In fact, verily, in many cases, gestures can cause emotions. Pascal

Blaise, a French mathematician, physicist, inventor, and writer, said, "Begin by kneeling and the mystical fervor will come by itself." In the same reasoning, the prophet Muhammad asked his followers to pray by bowing down to God five times a day. This is not because God requires that from us **but because it is a necessary gesture for mankind to surrender our egos.** This implicitly demonstrates the strength and hold of the ego over us. Similarly, the gesture can also often curtail an emotion. For example, a hand holding a cup of tea cannot slap something at the same time. In another example, the motion of anger will subside when its expression is impossible.

However, all of these arguments are not always necessarily decisive, because mimicry and bodily expression do not always trigger an authentic emotion. For instance, the expression of praying is subject to individual belief, mental and emotional state. Furthermore, Sacha Guitry, a French stage actor, film actor, and director, enriched this criticism by the following statement: "The talent of the actor consists in making the spectators feel emotions that he or she does not feel."

In general, the so-called emotion cannot be explained by the awareness of our organic disorders. Studies do not produce any evidence in support of James-Lange's thesis. On the contrary, an organic trouble followed by its awareness, for example, if our hands are trembling, this is not a solid and enough reason to provoke in us the emotion of fear (because they may be trembling out of cold). Therefore, it can be inferred that our perception of a particular moment in reality is not predominately grasped accurately, which is inhibited by our ability to acquire a comprehensive perspective towards understanding the entire story. Moreover, the James-Lange Theory neglects the role of tendencies excited by the representation, which is itself charged with meaning. For example, on a walk through the forest, my thoughts would impose on me the fear of possibly encountering a bear. However, I would not have any such thoughts of fear from contemplating a caged bear. Thus, while a caged bear would make me feel safe, a bear on the loose would imply for me a meaning of danger.

The intellectualist perspective:

In opposition to the physiological theory, the intellectualist theory reduces the emotion to the expression of a contradiction between two representations, i.e. of two ideas or thoughts. For example, yesterday I received excellent news from my friend René and then today I learned by chance that my friend René had passed away. Certainly in this case, my instinctive reaction would be a violent emotion. Hence, this contradiction between two representations can only be moving when it concerns my tendencies or my own system of values.

It has been correspondingly observed that intellectualists, like physiologists, neglect the role of tendencies. Thus, in the above example, if René was not my friend, this contradiction would not have caused in me a violent emotion. This, clearly, brings us back to and demonstrates a part of how we, as individuals, have a narrow field of consciousness. We fail to acquire an absolute infinite amount of information or data in order to infer a complete informative decision. Therefore, invariably, humans will always lack at least one or more parameters and thus, we always try to do our best to obtain the optimum results, using our available resources.

The psychophysiological perspective of Pierre Janet:

For Pierre Janet, emotion is a psychophysiological phenomenon with simultaneously psychic and organic disorders, especially of the central and secondary periphery. This means that the most important psychic disorders are disorders pertaining to the mental aspect, i.e. disorders of intelligence, language, memory, and superior acquisitions of the subject. Emotion is, therefore, a diminution of the mental level and capacity. Wherein, an individual uses primitive and elementary behavior due to his/her thoughts, reasoning and judgment being disturbed or agitated, while memory becomes incapable of evoking well-acquired memories.

It has been observed that language is also impacted in this case, and what is ordinarily correct becomes vulgar. For instance, my polite manners change to be the gross manners of a badly educated man. This is why emotion, for Janet, is perceived as a maladjusted behavior to a sudden and unexpected situation by which the subject is incapable of identifying a prompt answer. Thus, he responds to this situation with a primitive and maladjusted reaction.

According to Janet, emotion would thus be a global modification of behavior, which is understandable in the context of the dynamism of the system of tendencies. Therefore, it is essential for us to acquire self-knowledge and self-awareness to be able to master our emotions.

René Descartes' perspectives:

René Descartes insisted that the emotion is sourced from an overvaluation of the object. For example, if emerging successful in my examination is insignificant to me and I can perceive the failure without bitterness, then consequently I would take the exam calmly. However, if I accord much significance to the decisive nature of this examination with grave impact on my future, in this case, I risk being terribly stressed out.

Similarly, René Descartes also invited us to prevent emotional reactions while prescribing a prophylaxis that consists of subordinating the event to superior ideal values. For example, soldiers who are scared of the war, place high value on their own conservation. If it is possible to substitute this attachment to life with attachment to the fatherland, it will result in significant reduction or even disappearance of fear and panic in these soldiers.

The Paradox of Emotion

The emotion is a signal, which is loaded with meaning, yet this exact element helps an individual adapt to various situations. In the comprehensive study of the human psyche, it is imperative to underline the importance of this fact. Therefore, we can ask, if emotion is a function or a rout?

Some philosophers conceive of emotion as a function, and this is why they strive to emphasize the usefulness and purpose of emotional reactions.

Charles Darwin, an English naturalist, geologist, and biologist, stated that the preservation of emotion by natural selection could be essentially attributed to its utility. This defense mechanism helps mankind in our effort to adapt. For example, in anger, the upper lip rises and the individual becomes irritated and ready to bite. In fear, the eyes become enlarged and pupils better fixed on the dangerous object. Moreover, it acts as our internal compass and assist to navigates us to assess the preferred direction for our lives.

Walter Bradford Cannon, an American physiologist, professor, and chairman of the Department of Physiology at Harvard Medical School, insisted on a physiological fact. He argued that there is always a secretion of adrenaline by adrenal glands, which significantly impacts the fight or flight response in a threatening situation. This adrenaline is found in the blood during the emotion and acts on the muscles. Similarly, the sugar released by the liver makes the muscles stronger. Consequently, it can be inferred that physiological modifications will facilitate adaptation while in an emotional state.

Bergson said that it exists two levels of emotion: an infra-intellectual and a supra-intellectual emotion. These emotions enable scientists to appoint and propose a fruitful hypothesis, and heroes or saints have the necessary dynamism to renew or reinvent diverse moral ideas.

For Paul Ricoeur, a distinguished French philosopher of the twentieth century who was engaged in hermeneutical, phenomenological and psychoanalysis, emotion constitutes a source of action. It draws mankind from inertia but **it necessarily must be disciplined by the will**.

However, all these arguments are not decisive because emotion has always been considered a disorder, which disables us and paralyzes our reason, will, and body. In addition, it causes us to lose our self-control. Correspondingly, if emotional phenomena ever present us with some margin of adaptation, this adaptation will always remain incomplete. Emotion can never be accorded a finalist character as an instinct but is rather what the Swiss psychologist Jean Larguier des Bancels affirmed, "It is a spleen of the instinct because the instinct acts and the emotion agitates."

Emotion is a Disorder – A Rout

Charles Darwin established that emotions unadapt an individual. As such, these emotional reactions that formerly were useful with progression of time in different circumstances become absurd. Thus, with this projection, he rejected his own finalist theory. For example, when

I am furious, I stomp the ground. This stomping formerly presented a meaning and a utility. It was the stomping of the enemy. Today, it no longer embodies this character and therefore, the expression of such an emotion can imply a return to a primitive behavior.

Pierre Janet considered the emotion as a rout and analyzed it within the framework of his theory relative to the hierarchy of the conducts (i.e. inferior conduct and superior emotion/feeling). He distinguished between a higher regulating and a lower deregulatory behavior in the affective life. He inferred the feeling to be regulating and the emotion to be deregulatory. Feelings have a regulatory function comprehensively in everything that guides the conduct. Emotions, conversely, seem to present a disruptive function, causing uncontrolled and often inadequate conducts. An example of this would be a candidate who during an oral examination exhibits nervousness to the point where he/she cannot speak, and/or he/she begins to cry. What Pierre Janet wants us to understand is that emotion is a failure in behavior that causes the emotional being to lose his/her natural balance and clear perception, and prevents him/her from adapting to the situation. Consequently, under the effect of a strong moving emotion that inhibits the mental and organic functions, the emotional subject acts arbitrarily without any end, as if he/she is spending energy in vain.

Emotion is a Finalized Behavior

The viewpoint of Sartre proposed an original conception that deserves to be retained. For him, emotion is a conduct that is charged with meaning and constitutes a significant response to a given situation. In his book *Sketch for a Theory of Emotions*, he defined emotion as an adaptive behavior.

But what type or kind of adaptation is it?

He claimed that it is a magical adaptation of an "escape" behavior, which is dictated by the annihilating function of consciousness. In Sartre's emotion, **it is the body that is directed by consciousness, which changes its relations to the world so that the world changes our own qualities.**

I see a ferocious animal coming towards me, my legs tremble, my heart beats fast, and in fact nothing seems less adapted than this conduct that leaves me defenseless to danger. Yet I adapt myself magically, says Sartre, by conjuring an escape from reality through fainting. The fainting is therefore a refuge: Since I cannot physically remove the danger through an objective technique; I magically suppress it subjectively via changing my awareness of the danger. And this is the complexity of our emotions; they use us as much as we use them.

Sartre's perspective is concurrent with the orientation of all modern psychology. It conforms to the psychoanalytic explanations of the dream, the lapses, and the parapraxis, as it highlights a character of emotion neglected by classical psychology. Notably, emotion is a modification tool of beings in this physical world. However, while recognizing the frequent psychological significance of emotional reactions, we can only admit that emotion can be a true adaptation. However, it is rather a maladaptive adaptation, like the adaptation of people dying. For example, we are nearly insensitive to these grave occurrences since we have heard, saw, and read about these daily to the point that we became desensitized.

CHAPTER 6:

FEELING AND PASSION

Examples of feelings: triumph, satisfaction, joy, sadness, and more.

A feeling is the fixation of a tendency on an object. As described by Janet, feeling is a regulator of action; it is an organized reaction to a given situation. Similarly, for Maurice Pradine, feelings are functional reactions to a given situation, which are intended to regulate our specific conduct in accordance with that situation. Feelings are, therefore, essentially adaptive to a given situation. For instance, love is an attraction that precedes a pleasure.

The Values of Feelings

Our feelings accord the world a meaning – a value, which is why feelings are said to give a valorization to the world. Consequently, our feelings regulate our actions, providing the construct to establish our balance, an organized response to an organized situation.

Comparison between Feeling, Emotion, and Passion

Feeling	Emotion	Passion
Organize the world	A disorder that disorganizes	Organize a single object
Durable	Momentary	Durable
Establish an equilibrium	An imbalance	Equilibrium with respect to the object
Valorize the world	De-valorized	Valorize a single object and everything else is devalued

Definition of Passion

It is from feeling that we must define passion and not, as Ribot said, from emotion. Hence, we now attempt, in this section, to define passion from three perspectives: (i) from emotion, (ii) from the basis of feeling, and (iii) from tendencies.

From Emotion

Can we define passion based on emotion, as suggested by Ribot?

He said that passion "is a prolonged emotion." Or alternatively, it is an emotion that passes to the chronic state.

For Ribot, the difference between passion and emotion is not a difference of nature but a simple difference of degree, a difference between the momentary and the lasting. Apart from this difference, the passion process and the emotional process constitute the same progression, either in terms of their affective intensities or in terms of the upheaval they provoke.

This definition seems unfortunate, as the difference between emotion and passion cannot be so simplified. There is a specific difference that prevents us from defining one from the other. The logic in passion and coherence prevent us from confusing it with emotion because **emotion is a total upheaval of the personality and a sudden rupture of the human composer**. Assess the penny-pinchers, for example, who spend their time justifying their miserly existence, and think of means by which they can accumulate more wealth. Immanuel Kant, a German philosopher who is a central figure in modern philosophy, had grasped deftly the difference between passion and emotion to state, "**Emotion acts like a water that breaks the dike, passion like a torrent that digs its bedding more and more deep.**"

From the Basis of Feeling

It is, therefore, on the basis of feeling that one succeeds in defining passion.

Passion is a feeling that can be defined as exclusively tyrannical. However, essentially passion is more exalted and more ardent than feeling, and it transforms the world as it appears to us to facilitate seeing it in a new light. Yet it does it with excess, to the point that it blinds us to reality, causing disorder in our minds and behavior. Precisely by this fact it approaches emotion; however, in terms of being a relatively durable crisis, it presents a distinction. It can originate from an emotion and, in its turn, become a source of emotion. For example, love at first sight. **However, what makes passion is, above all, the preponderance and stability of a certain exalted tendency to the exclusion and detriment of the others. Thus, the true definition of passion must be based on tendencies. If a feeling can be defined as the fixation of a tendency on an object, how can one then define passion?**

From Tendencies

Henri Piéron, a French psychologist, defined passion as, "a predominantly exclusive and distorting tendency, exercising a directing influence on conduct and thought, controlling value judgments and preventing the exercise of an impartial logic."

According to this definition, passion plunges its roots into the subconscious psyche and in the world of tendencies. Therefore, the dynamism of passion is none other than that of tendency. Thus, the classification feasibility of passions can be safely inferred on the basis of tendencies.

Being virtual, the tendency remains largely indeterminate, while passion is a tendency that aims at a definite object. The need to love is a tendency, but the love of a specific person is an act of passion. For a tendency to evolve as a passion, it must be predominant, implying it must be developed in an exaggerated manner. Passion is also a generally exclusive tendency due to its attachment with a single object. Mankind cannot generally simultaneously express fully two great passions since passion has no rival within one being and one passion would dominates the other inadvertently.

Passion is also a distorting tendency because the exaggerated development of a tendency at the expense of all the others, leads to a distorted reality and to a detrimental perception of it. It deforms a person's reality by enriching a single object and impoverishing all the others. For this, an average woman appears to be divine in the eyes of her lover. This deformation is explained by a theme brought by Stendhal, a French writer, which is the crystallization, "A random branch, thrown into a basin of salt; when removed it is all splendid filled with crystals."

Such is the case of the object of our passion − an object to which we attribute all possible values and qualities. Correspondingly, the gambler ignores his/her financial ruin and the desperate lover does not think of his/her dishonor. It is essential to note that passion exercises a direct influence on conduct and thought, discounting a balanced behavior, with a thought process, which is not critical and coherent. The passionate person reflects, calculates, and thinks however unlike others he/she thinks much more like a normal individual possessing a kind of a weakness.

Gifted with a very great imagination, the passionates are able to justify everything and these hypersensitive beings perceive the world through the object of their passion. "I hear your voice in all the world's noise," wrote the French poet Alphonse de Lamartine. The passionates are also hypermetric beings with a robust memory of all the details and all the events concerning the object of their passion. But they are also amnesiacs, in a certain sense, as they present a tendency to forget things like the faults of loved ones, as they possess the quality of forgiving very quickly.

Passion commands the judgment of value and prevents the exercise of an impartial logic. Indeed, the passion logic is not the rational logic but rather the logic of the heart, which prevents the passionates from true reality or an accurate perception. And if the passionates are active types, their activity is not always the product of a reflexive synthesis because they summarily discount all the elements and all of the moments. The passionates are people of a single instinct and for a single instant. Alternatively, autonomous people succeed in effecting a reflexive synthesis, and present the capability to find harmony between the different elements, with a generic opposition to passion. For this, the will and the passion seem to oppose each other, just as freedom and slavery are in opposition. Particularly, evident in the case of the exalted passions, wherein the individual perseveres despite of him/herself.

The Genesis of Passion

How is a tendency exaggerated to the point of becoming a passion?

Via six different ways:

1. Through an external event leaving only an ephemeral impression on us, passion presents a solid support.

2. Through organic conditions like temperament, which can bring congenital dispositions to passion. There are temperaments predisposed to jealousy and others to drunkenness.

3. Through desire, which is the seed of passion; it requires a prior representation of the purpose of the act regarding the desired object. Consequent to this representation, results the seed of passion and the imagination imposes this object with all kinds of qualities. This is what is called, in the language of Stendhal, the "crystallization of passion." Correspondingly, the vital role of the imagination effects the possibility of an excessive and exclusive development of a tendency. The participation of the imagination is a fundamental element in passion.

4. Through the environment, under its triple aspects: physical, social, and moral, which all impact the genesis of passion.

The physical environment – The climate, the temperature, and the material wealth, all can favor the development of an ex-inclination: The city environment for example is more favorable to the outbreaks of carnal love than small town or remote areas. The cause is in the motivations propelling the individual towards a person of the other (or same) sex, such as the diverse availabilities of social activities like attending to a theater, eating in restaurant, clubbing/dancing, meeting on a train or in shopping malls, etc.

The social environment – Every society, each current period, and each social group present specific individual passions. There is indeed a contagion for passions and correspondingly as we observe history or timelines, a privileged and favorable atmosphere for certain passions during certain periods is evident.

The moral environment – This also plays an important role in the development of the seed of passion. Prohibitions, moral and religious imperatives, and the judgments of values, which dominate the individual from birth (They vary from one society to another), all favor the exaggerated development of a tendency. But, above all, it is the psychological aspects that significantly impact the birth of passions. Passion, as it was affirmed by psychoanalysis, originated in the subconscious. French philosopher Ferdinand Alquié once said, "Passion results from a transfer of compensation or sublimation."

5. From a transfer: The passionate draw on the object of their passion past and forgotten memories, which continue to dominate them subconsciously.

6. Via compensation: Passion can also be the sublimation of a frustrated desire. Thus, the passion at the mystical level is the sublimation of a frustrated human love. In the same way, passion can sometimes be a response to an anguish, which finds its clear meaning only in our past events. In another way, passion always expresses an image and a symbol of a past reality.

The Object of Passion

- It can be one thing: Money, stamps, tobacco, drugs, etc.
- It can be a person: Love, jealousy, etc.
- It can be an ideal: The beautiful, the good, the real, etc.
- Or it can be an idea: Freedom, justice, peace, power, etc.

Value of Passion

Moralists condemning passion perceived it singularly to be entirely negative, i.e. to induce in us disorder and imbalance. Kant saw in passion a real disease of the soul and rather, passion is revealed as a partial and biased valorization of the world. Herein, specifically, one single feeling is enriched excessively to the detriment of other neglected feelings. Passion can also limit us in space and time. In space, because it causes a reduction in our field of consciousness together with our interests to a single object and in time because it makes us prisoners of the present or the past.

The passionates are individuals who, in some way, are cut off from reality. In the absence of the object of their passion, they feel lost; they can no longer adapt to the real situations in life. Hence, every passion sooner or later leads the individual to misfortune. Moreover, the passionate are not the master of their own actions and present a partial or biased awareness of the selves. **It is not the person that is the master of his/her act; rather, the subconscious complexes, while autonomous people act according to their whole personality.** They lucidly prioritize their tendencies and take into account all the moments of time. In addition, passion is a source of selfishness due to its urgent need for possession that it reveals with regard to its object.

While considering the negative aspect that the Moralists have seen in passion, we cannot neglect alternatively the exalting positive aspect of the Romantics. According to them, passion breaks the monotony of the everyday life and it gives value to existence. "Nothing great in the world was accomplished without passion," says Georg Wilhelm Friedrich Hegel. Passion, according to the Romantics, sources the powerful motives underlying all our actions and creations. It is also the outcome of all actions executed by our will. Moreover, it is passion that allows a person to resonate in the world and taste the pleasures of life.

However, for a good understanding of passion, it is necessary for us to operate a multitude of distinctions between passions and values. To begin, we consider those directed towards values of less selfish nature than sensual passions and secondly, with sole objective of the possession of their object. Even these first would be a source of disequilibrium if the subject neglects other feelings, for here again passion presents an exclusive role. The passionate individual knows neither family nor sentiment nor duty to feel pity, and so there are noble passions equally as the inferior passions. Even a feeling such as maternal love, when it becomes a passion, it changes into a desire for possession or spiritual domination. Of course, the ideal evident path would be to guard ourselves against exaggerated passions to maintain our desires within the right balanced limits.

Pierre Janet noticed that passion generally result from periods of moral depression, boredom, or idleness. If correctly diagnosed and identified at this stage, it is possible for an individual to recover himself or herself by avoiding such abdications of the will.

The Fight Against Problematic Passions

How can we free ourselves from problematic passions?

Our power over passion is rather restricted because it transforms our personality, distorts our intelligence, alters our sensibility, and subjugates our normal will. How, then, can we expect a subject with a polarized entire psychic life to recover from his/her passion?

Fortunately, it happens that external incidents (such as the attitude of the entourage, the implications of consequences, and errors committed or moral scruples) contribute, even though momentarily, towards the revelation of reality to the passionate. In certain cases, it is difficult and can be even dangerous to seek to fight against the passion directly, as the attempt would conversely only result in stabilizing its strength. It is therefore necessary to fight passion indirectly.

Our real power is to seek to distract ourselves, to escape the universe that imprisons us, and to leave for the so-called change of air or change of environment. It happens then that the passion rapidly fades away, and a sudden de-crystallization occurs.

Because passion is an imbalance, one can also try to restore balance by constraining oneself to physical activities like sports — if that passion was not in this domain (the idea is to indulge in activities that have nothing to do with the current passion).

However, the most flexible therapy is the one presented by psychoanalysis. It is a question of exploiting the passionate impulse by directing it towards other less egoistic objectives and more beneficial goals for the self as well as the community. This method would involve lucidity and knowledge of oneself, thereby propelling us to sublimate the passionate energy by inverting it in an ideal superior world. For example, one can cure passion through a new preoccupation – by work that is of creative source – because idleness or laziness is a very bad and inimical state of being. When the subject sinks into profitable and serious work, he/she will gradually forget his/her problematic passion.

Finally, it is essential to note that it is impossible to strip the passionate impulse in a single stroke. **This affair presupposes a great effort and time just like everything else in life.**

CHAPTER 7:

THE WILL

"Freedom (free will), one might call the Divinity of Humanity. It is the most beautiful, the most superb, the most irrevocable of all of the Creator's gifts to us. The Supreme Creator will not violate this Freedom without denying its own nature." Said the French occult author Eliphas Levi.

The act of will is an intentional act, preceded by a conscious project and determined by the representation of its consequences. Jean-Paul Sartre said, "A heavy smoker who inadvertently explodes an ashtray has not acted, his act is not out of will. On the other hand, a worker who is in charge with dynamiting a passage, and who obeyed the orders given to him. Thus, when the explosion was provoked, his act was out of will. The worker knew what he was doing." The will act carries the mark of the ego. Mankind recognizes themselves in their will acts, for which we are responsible.

Classical Schema of the Will Act

Traditionally, the act of will has been divided into four stages:

1st – The conception of a project: It is the representation of the objective.

2nd – Deliberation: It is a discussion with oneself where we weigh and assess the pros and cons, or analyze the motives and reasons.

3rd – The decision: It is the will "fact" to agree with what I already know.

4th – Execution: This is the practical application of the decision.

French philosopher Maurice Blondel criticized this pattern terming it artificial. Likewise, Jean Paul Sartre argued that the decision-making step occurs before deliberation. Today, in modern psychology, we do not deny that the will act essentially presents a dramatic element, or there are conceptions, deliberation, decisions, and execution. Yet we are not limited to this chronology imposed by the traditional school schema.

The Problems of the Nature of Willpower

The Intellectualist Perspectives

The Intellectualist perspectives which link religiousness to a need to understand and control the world limits the act of will to the first two stages cited, as in the classical schema of the Intellectualist theories. Thus, for the Dutch philosopher Baruch Spinoza, a clear idea imposes itself and a decision out of will results singularly from the power of the idea. Optimally, the idea is clear and obvious for a passion to pass immediately to the act. And if ever we are in doubt, or our indecisiveness can be attributed to lack of clarity in the ideas supporting our thesis. Spinoza starts from the example, which he declared arbitrary, that the evidence of a theorem in mathematics imposes the decision. It is, therefore, sufficient for Intellectualists to be rationally convinced of the purpose for will action.

Simply a conceived conviction of clear execution is insufficient. For example, I can be convinced of the danger of cigarettes but this conviction does not imply that I will quit smoking. As well as I can be convinced of a political party and yet not engage in that party.

It is true that the will act requires reflection and deliberation. However, these conditions singularly are limited in psychic illnesses of the will – nothing more typical than the abulia – as the patient reasons and reasons too much. Then the patient weighs the pros and cons, and ultimately he/she progresses to be incapable of execution. Similarly, one cannot confine the act of will exclusively to the decision because it often happens to me to decide without passing from decision to the act. The decision knows itself as a decision only by executing it – that is, including itself in the material worlds and among obstacles.

Correspondingly, Paul Valery, a French philosopher and poet, wrote, "I will tear this letter, then out of another opinion, I file it instead." It is, therefore, the execution that makes the authenticity of the act of will.

To affirm is not to act; the key to wanting is at the level of execution.

Let us add that the Intellectualist proposition acknowledges the predominance of reason, while concurrently projecting a neglect of our tendencies, needs, and desires. It is true that reason plays a great part because the act of will is at first a reflective act, but reason alone is not enough. Pascal Blaise said, **"Reason does not know how to put the price on things." Thus, it is desire that essentially, places a price on them.** For these reasons, one should not settle in life, as settling disrupts your desires expressions and for them to potentially be activated to emerge through the layers of consciousness necessary for the will to develop them. That said, desire is unable to autonomously fructify without the appreciation of your current possessions. Once I develop a desire, then reason may teach me how to realize it as well as valuing it.

Reason cannot set the ends and invents only the means to realize them. Tendencies are the only way to set these ends.

Empiricist Perspectives of Condillac

In opposition to the Intellectualist proposition, which neglects the role of tendencies and desires, Condillac brings back the will to the power of an exclusive desire. The realizable is the exclusive desire and the excitation, which results from a conflict between several desires culminating in the predominance of a single decision. This is the existence of a single desire in the field of our consciousness.

Therefore, in order to understand this perspective, should a distinction be made between desire and will?

Desire is quite different from will; it is a simple wish that may be even unrealizable and a dream absent of an operative technique. Whereas a will requires the courage to perform an act, in fact, it embodies the great effort to manifest for us our opus. "There is no will but by a power that incarnates it." For example, a mother with a son going away to war may desire his return but she cannot want it as the return does not depend on her. Furthermore, she may want to send her son a package as this proposition presents an immediate possibility.

Alternatively, desire is a pure impulse, whereas the will is a mastery of oneself. Desire is not an action. It is a dream, it is a prayer, and it is of the order of the instant of caprice. While, will is work, it has the sense of what is real, and so it says "no" to fantasies and to utopias.

Similarly, desire presents a sociological and characterological physiological weight; while the will, on the contrary, is a power to escape from these determinants.

The world of a child is that of desires, whereas the world of the adult constitutes of will and work. And attributing to these reasons, the will can only relate to immediate acts, inserted in the present. Therefore, it is said that the will exists only in execution, whereas a desire always concerns a future that escapes us.

There is no will without a technique and these techniques construct our individual set of habits and acquired knowledge. Correspondingly, in the absence of will, the power of my body is my instrument of insertion and actions into the world. The incarnation of our wills projects easily, owing to our habits and our acquired know-how. For these reasons, for example, there is a fundamental difference between the desire to overcome shyness that requires a sophisticated dive into the psyche or to develop the will to learn to swim, which requires an action from the individual. Condillac admitted that there is only will in the achievable desire. But with an absolute desire, Condillac acknowledged, even if it is achievable, it cannot be confused with will.

The role of the affective phenomena in the constitutions of an act of will is indisputable and the contribution of the Empiricist perspectives are definitely considerable. **If will is an activity, it is undoubtedly rooted in the world of tendencies, needs, and desires.**

Desire indeed constitutes the indispensable tool to the psychology of will, but if we were to reduce the act of will to the force of desire, it would be an act of error because an exclusive or absolute desire does not deserve the name of will. Rather, it pertains to the question of a passionate impulse. The passionate individual is the victim of a mental vertigo, whereas the will presupposes the clear conception of the goal, or more specifically the lucidity of consciousness. An individual who utilizes will is the one who is the master of his/her desires and thus is able to resist the forces of these desires. This is what made Charles Renouvier, a French philosopher, say, "to really want, is to want what one does not want," (or, in other terms, that one does not desire). To present the conscious use of will is to be able to stop or inhibit the impulse of desire to have time for self-restriction or control. Particularly, to face the conflicts of individual desires that disturbs the core of our being. The will is, therefore, a power to overcome obstacles in an effort to subdue its impulses, and willpower is the mastery of will.

The energy of desire is sourced from an act of will, enlightened exclusively via intelligence. Correspondingly, any attempt to analyze its purpose leads to confusion amongst an individual's presented tendencies. The act of will is therefore neither gratuitous nor arbitrary.

The Definitions of Will
(Wanting to Want)

The French philosopher Maine de Biran defined will as a hyper-organic force in relation to a living resistance, which is proved best in the muscular effort. For example, I raise a chair with an outstretched arm, and this action is followed by instant pain in my arm. Although, if I want, I can continue my effort. Therefore, I am not only this body but also the higher will to the body.

William James has defined will as an indefinite additional force that can be increased or decreased by an individual, i.e. a psychic act; a mental and conscious effort. The effort does not relate to my mechanically carried out bodily gestures and involves meritorious representations. My body is an epiphenomenon that is quite an accessory.

What is difficult is not the muscular and mechanical act of leaving the bed on a winter day but to make the decision, keep it in our consciousness, and to exclude laziness from it. For a king, muscular effort to sign his abdication is minimal, meaning that the difficulty is to accept the idea of abdication.

However, the painful sensations, which result from bodily sensations and sensitivities, are very hard to bear. For example, an individual who commits suicide with a revolver may renounce this act if he/she knows how to use a scalpel or a blade. Correspondingly, Maine de Birau, presents a unique accuracy in not disregarding the relationships of the body and the will. However, what is this ultimate power that says "I want" and that resists desire?

William James said, "Will is a fiat, a pure power to say 'yes' or 'no' to this desire or to this idea that crosses my mind." This perspective corroborates a very famous theme of the Cartesian philosophy from Descartes, which attributes to mankind an infinite will, sourced from the original creation. Therefore, as a free will being, we decide our individual use of it.

Such will is completely disembodied; it is the constraint of desire. **This will is a free decision – a transcendent faculty and a pure power to say "yes" or "no," "to do" or "not to do."** I want it because I want it. It is a metaphysical free will, which is beyond all psychological explanation.

The Paradox of the Explanation of the Will

The Swiss neurologist and child psychologist Édouard Claparède reduced the act of will to a mechanical outcome of our desires. The strongest desires will trigger the decision and result in the execution. This is evident in the simple explanation that a crime is committed because the desire to kill is stronger than the fear of imprisonment.

His definition joins that of Condillac, which states that we no longer perceive the distinction between the act of will and the indecision act (non-will). Correspondingly, psychological determinism annihilated the notion of the will.

Such is the paradox of the will: Either I discover at the root level of my free will the determinism of my desire to act, and therefore the notion of will would disappear... or I define the will as a transcendent faculty outside of tendencies, and then I am no longer just a ghost of will.

The Findings of Bergson

For Bergson, the acts of will are formed and developed in a continuous period, wherein the elements of the personalities (feelings, desires, ideas, aspirations, etc.) do not appear successively to consciousness (each with its own power although they are all interacting). In addition, the acts of will are precisely the result and the fruit of this interaction. **An act can be said to be of will only if it emanates from the totality of the personality – only if it expresses it entirely.**

This idea of totality contradicts the essential character of the will, which is division and sacrifice. The act of will supposes a choice and, therefore, entails a sacrifice. One always sacrifices a part of oneself that would have been abandoned and abdicated.

This conception of Bergson's is naturally formed and appears as a mechanical result of the elements of the personality. However, is it still possible to speak of will? Isn't the confusion between the will and indecision (non-will) evident? Is the decision still mine when it is done in me? And without me? What is this act of will? And what are the elements necessary for a correct definition of will?

The Accepted Concept of Will by Most Modern Psychologists

The will, which is not a mysterious faculty, imposes itself without any modification and thus, should not be confused with pure intelligence. It is not reduced to the sum of the tendencies, yet there is no will without a system of tendencies, without intelligence and reflection. In fact, the act of will produces a reflective synthesis of tendencies for actions in the world.

The will is opposed to the impulse and an individual acting with will does not necessarily yield to the first solicitations, which present themselves between a given situation and the reaction executed.

There is room for consciousness to reflect, and this reflection itself, contains the choice, as well as the considerations of all possibilities. Individuals that utilize their will, attributed to individual reasoning and reflection, can express their total personality. This is because, in choosing, their choice is not absolute but solicited from a certain nature. This, in turn, can be a certain past, a certain present, and a certain culture or environment. To act out of will is to know what one wants in order to become aware of the fundamental requirements of one's person, to renounce and to satisfy such desires; this may be agile but contradictory with the reasons to act.

Likewise, the will is complete only when it is completed in an intelligent execution. I, when therefore place all my person in the act of will, I recognize myself there.

The individual that practices will reacts to its motives with a moment of pause and deliberation. Yes, we hesitate, but this hesitation does not pertain to the project itself but rather to ourselves. The will relies on a value table, a hierarchy. For example, the ideal to which a volunteer ascribes gives him/her a course of action. Thus, the will appears as a regulating function, according to the French philosopher André Darbon, wherein mankind continues to work despite being tired. Similarly, people will smile when sad and remain courteous when angry.

According to Maurice Blondel, the value table on which the will is based is of the social origin. It is the social solicitations that construct the acts of will. The social appears in almost all acts of mankind. For example, it is not well regarded to yawn in a meeting, and it's not comfortable to leave a warm bed on an icy cold day. Conversely, though, every table of values is not necessarily of social origin, and occasions of revolt against established collective consensuses are also evident.

And with the assertion: The problem of the origin of values escapes psychology, we shall abandon it, and assert that **the will of mankind is always an ideal that gives meaning our lives, that allows us to discipline our tendencies and consequently to acquire self-mastery.**

The act of will is characterized as:

- Intentional
- Reflected
- Rational
- Dynamic
- Free
- Personal
- Existential

The "id" is realized by acting willingly or on a voluntarily basis.

Pathology of Will

The act of will presents itself as a synthesis of our reason, for our motivations, and our means of action. And correspondingly, it would bring into play our whole personality, which is why a disease of the will is also a disease of the personality.

We can distinguish different levels:

- Suggestibility – At this stage the tendency undergoes an extreme external influence. Here, others dominate the individual and the individual is limited from acting on his/her free will.

- The desire or intention – Herein, the will to act does not get necessarily translated into an act of will. At this stage, an individual starts several projects but fails to finish any.

- The caprice – This refers to the situation when the individual acts in a fantastical way and quite often results from an education that lacks authority. This is exemplified in the behavior of some parents in bending to their caprices or whims, in order to do what is good for their child and avoid any kind of complexity.

- The scruple – At this stage, an individual is prevented from performing an action due to the underlying fear of the associated consequences.

- The obstinacy and the spirit of contradiction – This state presents itself as a fixation in the stage of negativism. Here an individual opposes him/herself.

- Abulia – At this level, the individuals are characterized by their irresolution abilities, particularly they think indefinitely without acting.

- Bulimia – This consists of undertaking everything without realizing anything; and is termed as a bulimia (disorder) of will. A Spanish proverb epitomizes this: "Who grasps all, loses all."

Education of Will

Will involves a mastery and self-control, which is acquired through the following formative education:

- Physical education – This pertains to the primary school of will, exemplified in the phrase "Healthy mind in the healthy body."

- Emotional or feeling education – It consists of avoiding passions and associated ties of the human being to function optimally and adopt superior values.

- Education of intelligence – This is best explained via a quote from Descartes: "A great clarity in the understanding follows a great inclination in the will."

- Spirit of discipline – To be able to command, you must first learn to obey.

CHAPTER 8:

THE SIMPLE AND THE CONDITIONAL REFLEX

Nature of Reflex

The reflex is an automatic reaction of nervous activity, which is characterized by the close correlation that makes a response dependent on a determined stimulus. And, attributing to this reason, it is opposed to the act of will.

The reflex is presented either as a limited or simple response provoked by an external stimulation. For example, the patellar reflex, also called the knee-jerk reflex, involves a sudden kicking movement of the lower leg, which occurs in response to a sharp tap on the patellar tendon. The reflex can also be a reactive element in a complex behavior (for example, the self-protection and the defense reflex) or as an element of an apathetic regulation (for example, the glandular secretion aspects, secretions of saliva, gastric juice, and adrenaline).

Characteristics of Reflexes

The reflexive reaction to a specific stimulation, is, therefore, a phenomenon that is:

- Simple
- Purely Physiological
- Unchangeable
- Necessary and inevitable
- Immediate and triggered automatically by a stimuli

Two Types of Reflex Classifications

The simple natural reflex is spontaneous and innate.

The conditional reflex is a reflex acquired by conditioning.

Pavlov, essentially discovered the mechanism; and the discovery came about, when he noticed that a dog was salivating not only at the sight of food but also at any sign or indication that would announce the meal. Although, this sign had to be conditioned to be frequently associated with the perception of food. The reinforcement of the conditional reflex is obtained through establishing an association between the two normal and conditioned stimuli applied successively. The extinction of the conditional reflex is obtained by deconditioning (i.e. by the repeated application of conditioned stimulus to accompany the normal stimulus).

Correspondingly, such conditioning not only is operative for animals, but also for humans. Therefore, this projects the feasibility of conditioning and training the human brain to function in a certain way.

Even though you think that your reactions, beliefs, and thoughts belong singularly to you; this is a false conception as everything is acquired from our surrounding environment.

Practical Value of the Conditional Reflex

There are three principles that need to be considered:

1. **Principle of animal training** – A dog would immediately go in search of a ball that you just threw, attributing to the learned associations. At the initial training period of dogs, they are taught to associate the sounds of the word "approach" plus the word of pursuit "fetch", which presents the link that condition their training. In addition, it also marks their association between the execution of the act and a reward for the dog.

2. **Principle of education** – Similar associations can be obtained in the child by the same technique. For the child, the word "bell" can be a signal or a notification of something, analogous to the indication of the bell, as meant for the dog. During the training process, instinctive satisfactions are gradually replaced by symbolic satisfactions. These can be obtained by indirect means to the normal stimulus, which is substituted by a conditional stimulus. For example, the need for escape can be satisfied by daydreams or through reading a fictional novel.

3. **Principle of learning** – Complex conscious behaviors can be introduced and subsequently obtained by conditioning and can also be reduced to simple conditional reflexes. Some examples include riding a bicycle, typing, and reacting to specific signals.

CHAPTER 9:

INSTINCT

The first question that might come to mind is: **Does mankind have instincts?**

The word "instinct" is an equivocal term, which conveys two very different meanings.

In the vocabulary of the active life, the word "instinct" designates an innate know-how, which is evidenced in the example of bees presenting default knowledge of making honey or building cells and conversely, in this definition mankind presents no such instinct.

In the vocabulary of the affective life, "instinct" refers to the tendency or inclination that dominates the whole psychic life (for example, the sexual, social, artistic tendency, etc.). Unlike the example as explained in the animal, these instincts in mankind do not present an innate know-how. The only singular example of an innate know-how in mankind would pertain to the newborn's act of suckling. Tendencies require learning and, with that, correspondingly, the role of intelligence cannot be neglected. In fact, it is the element of intelligence that will subsequently invent the techniques to satisfy them. In mankind, instinct is thus reduced to the tendency and to the drive.

We can, therefore, come to the following definition: "Instinct" refers to a set of reactions of the living organism towards definite external factors, and it presents itself as complex reflexes. These reflexes present the qualities of being innate, natural, and specific, always responding to determined stimuli and their characters of stability and perfection. During the individual existence, these reflexes can be supplemented by the acquisition of conditional reflexes. Hence, certain flexibility with an adaptation of the instinct is a progress possibility, even in an animal.

Classical Analysis of the Characteristics of Instinct and Traditional Opposition between Instinct and Intelligence

Instinctive behavior and intelligent behavior appear to have objectives and these subordinated acts as regards the goals present a means to an end, such as the swallow that builds its nest and the mason who builds a house. In this example, the acts that are necessary to build the nest have a meaning, though they are not conscious and thoughtful acts. Correspondingly, instinctive behavior is distinguished via essential points of intelligent behavior.

The instinct is innate. A bee inherently is a domestic and nourishing insect, which later becomes a constructor of cells. Herein the associated activities are innate to the extent that they do not require learning and appear from the maturation of certain glands. Specifically, intelligent activities require trial and error, research, and learning. The potential mental and intellectual capacity are hereditary but present the basic need to be developed. Conversely, intelligence-acquired activities are not transmitted through genetics.

The instinct is immutable. The entire techniques of intelligence have been discovered by individuals. Therefore, imitating and teaching of these techniques is strategized through trials and errors. These techniques always have a progressive graph because errors can be rectified. Thus, the instinctive know-how is immutable and the progress is limited or absent when there are no errors and mistakes. Adaptation towards the ends exists in a perfect way.

The rigid instinct is blind. For example, when a wasp lays its eggs, it constructs cells for them to provide housing. And to cater to the food need, it catches caterpillars and paralyzes them by stinging them at the nervous ganglia. Then it deposits the caterpillars in the cells before sealing them. On hatching, the larvae will find a supply of food in these paralyzed caterpillars. If someone or something pierces any of these cells that the wasp has built, it will simply neglect to clog the breach. It has been observed that the wasp would usually discover the hole and explore it with its antennas but continue without making repairs. These rigid instinct operations became absurd, which glaringly present a contrast to the suppleness and plasticity of intelligence. For example, when masons notice damage in the construction of the building, they would acknowledge it, repair it, and adapt to the altered situation through different measures. Herein, thus, the masons will have exceeded the difficulty that has arisen to them.

The Most Prominent Findings

According to Bergson, there is an essential opposition, which is evident between instinct and intelligence. These fundamentally are two finalized but divergent solutions.

Instinct is an essential element of life, and correspondingly, our vital momentum is aimed towards achieving a resolution of the problem of adaptation by two methods: through instinct and intelligence.

The instinct is a natural instrument in the animal, which is a part of the body and every instinctive function corresponds to an organ. The biological organization in the animal is prolonged in the instinct that uses the organs.

An organism (a person or an animal), does not naturally have all the necessary tools in life, however, intelligence causes the vital impulses to act and create them. For example, an individual deprived of clothes, via intelligence, has the ability to create other solutions to resolve the issue. There is, then, a superiority manifestation of intelligence over instinct; instinct is a preformed path. Intellect makes a retreat to organize matter and choose its processes. Therefore it uses consciousness. Instinct is blind – it is implied – while intelligence is universal, flexible, and leaves the door open to progress.

But in an alternative perspective, instinct is superior to intelligence, external to its object. Intelligence remains on the surface of things as it attracts the object towards it through the use of abstraction analysis and symbolization. It does not present the singular and concrete realities. The instinctive knowledge, according to Bergson, seizes very little information, however it stems from within the organism. Correspondingly, consciousness is lived and not represented. There is sympathy between the sphex and its victim, as it informs it from within where to direct the sting.

To Bergson, this perfect knowledge or innate know-how is nothing but intuitive: There is both a clairvoyance of intelligence and a direct contact with the object it meets. This analysis is termed by Bergson as the "theory of sympathetic instinct."

This analysis needs to be further discussed, as the infallibility of instinct is contested and presents a metaphysical thesis that seems quite gratuitous. However, the connection between instinct and life is to be accounted in Bergson's explanation because the instinctive behavior prolongs the biological organization and can be assimilated to a biological function.

According to the mechanistic perspectives on instinct (instinct and reflex), to study the instinct scientifically, it would be necessary to analyze it and to decompose it into a simple element. Therefore, the main question is: **Can instinct be reduced to rigorously determined mechanisms?**

Descartes thought that animal behavior resembled the movements of machinery, i.e. machines that respond by movements to a limited number of situations. Animal behavior, is, therefore an adaptation to a narrow specialization, which is a limited, and specialized register of reactions. Likewise, the animals act by the disposition of their organs.

Furthermore, the mechanistic thesis refuses instinct to reflex. Specifically, the reflex is an automatic, motor-driven response to an extreme stimulus. However, instinct, says Étienne Rabaud, a French zoologist, "is a chain of reflexes."

The key to instinct is the extreme stimulus that springs from it. Correspondingly, Rabaud exemplifies this phenomenon through the example of the spider that first builds its web and the rushes on its prey when the web vibrates. Thus, in case the branches of the tuning forks were inserted in its web, the spider would be able react in advance to the vibrations as if it had caught its prey.

In another observation, we can cite yet one more example of migratory birds that, when exposed to a regularly growing light, headed north (and when exposed to a gradually decreasing light, headed south).

Thus, clearly, in this case, the instinctive behavior is triggered by an external stimulus, which is exposure to light.

However, the mechanistic perspective can no longer assimilate instinct with an elementary reflex. Karl von Frisch, an Austrian ethologist, and Konrad Lorenze, an Austrian zoologist, ethologist, and ornithologist, consider internal motivations to be more important than the external stimulus. The specific behavior of the instinct is explained not by a hormonal secretion but by a complex hereditary disposition, which is inscribed in the nervous system of the animal. Similarly, the external stimulus trigger is not an isolated element but is a configuration of elements. The reflex is understood only in terms of the overall state of the organism. The animal is a living being, and its behavior will always be influenced by its internal motivations. For example, the female mammal is sensitized to the male only in period of "heat", which marks the reproductive season.

Alternatively, Lorenze concluded that the impregnation phenomenon in ducklings occurs in so far as much as the animal is motivated to follow any mobile body that emits sounds a few hours after its birth. Correspondingly, even though the instinctive behavior can be reduced to a certain extent to mechanisms, these mechanisms primarily indicate the service of an end – it is the adaptation of the animal. There is then finality for the instinct.

The theory of instinct and habit was, in fact, proposed by Lamarck, who asserted that instinctive behavior originated in a habit acquired by ancestors and was then transmitted through heredity. For example, if an experimenter approaches a small butterfly with the flame of a candle, the insect will move its antennae backwards. However, if the flame of the candle comes from behind, the insect still carries its antennas behind and the antennae get burnt. It is not a question here of the rigidity of an innate instinct. Thus, for a newly hatched butterfly, according to this observation, instead of referring to an innate instinct, we should refer to a habit, as the butterfly in its natural environment is conditioned to face obstacles that present themselves from the front. The insect starts to learn the habit of projecting its antennas back on the approach of danger.

Moreover, according to the Chinese experimental and physiological psychologist Zind-Yang Kuo, we can indeed by habit affect a change some instinctive behaviors. For example, a kitten raised with mice does not present a predatory behavior towards them.

However, these theories that reduce instinct to the habit seem debatable. Indeed, science has just begin to get a glimpse of and to demonstrate the heredity of acquired traits. Alternatively, on observation, it has been evidenced that a cat raised with mice does not attack them individually, while it predates on other rodents.

Is Instinct Moldable and Educable? Can it be Brought Closer to Intelligence?

There is an apparent link between instinct and intelligence. We sometimes notice in certain instinctive behaviors a flexibility or an adaptation to the circumstances, as well as a finality, i.e. pertaining more to intelligence. For example, some birds construct nests of different shapes according to the foliage of the tree.

Increasingly, the scientists have begun to acknowledge the existence of intelligence in the animal world, especially while observing ravens that are taught to make a pulley using a stick, to raise seeds from a hole. While in the tufted trees, birds construct nests that are broad and flat; in other trees, the nests are narrow and deep.

Similarly, scientists have also noticed that canaries released from their cages first made nests that looked very awkward, but over time, eventually perfected their technique. The sphex seems to want to paralyze the cricket to ensure fresh food to its young. However, the nature of all these similarities is superficial. As the sphex is unaware of its actions and it does not establish the relationship between the means and the ends. It acts instinctively and dies before its eggs actually hatch.

Likewise, if the canaries seem to make progress in their techniques instinctively, the first nest they make is specific. It is true that instinct presents the characteristics of being (i) partially educable (like the previous example of the kitten raised with mice), (ii) sometimes flexible, and (iii) its rigidity is not always absolute. There is sometimes the possibility of an adaptation. For example, in hot countries, the bee does not make provisions for honey. Its instinct is then relatively moldable, which proves the neuroplasticity, later discussed in the book.

Moreover, instinct presents a small provision for learning by conditioning. For example, Von Fish in his experience with bees, advised farmers to paint their hives in various colors so that the bees can better detect their hive during their flight.

But instinctive behavior is always different from intelligent behavior. This is why, instead of opposing intelligence and instinct, we consider them to pertain to different levels of seemingly complementary behavior at the level of the unity of living beings.

The instinct always remains an innate know-how, which is not satisfied with innate techniques and which depends on the maturation of the organs. This final inherent knowledge allows the solution of the problems. The intelligent act, too, is finalized, but the intelligence projects the result of the act that it wants to accomplish and executes it taking into account this desired end, which is why mankind is called "the being of the distant," as said by Martin Heidegger, a German philosopher. The intelligent act is progressive (i.e. guided by the image of the consequences of its action), whereas instinct ignores what it prepares itself. **Instinct is there when there is no consciousness towards ends.**

Intelligence prolongs instinct; and perfects itself by choosing the appropriate means to realize the ends. It replaces the rigid adaptation of instinct with a flexible adaptation. Particularly, intelligence supposes consciousness of the relations between means and ends. In instinct, the value or the purpose of the act is ignored and refers to a cycle where the elements participate only subconsciously in the achievement of the goal.

This human form of intelligence is not the only possible form and in addition, there is an obscure, global, animalistic form that presents a rudimentary existence in the insect and more noticeably in the superior animal kingdom. This animal intelligence is distinguished from that of mankind by the absence of abstraction, a concept that allows the development and emergence of language.

Hence, what is Instinct?

Instinct is a fortuitous association of reflexes and habits. It is subordinate to the interest of the species. Correspondingly, Lalande said that instinct is "a complex set of determined external reactions commonly hereditary to all the individuals of the same species and adapted towards a goal where the living being acting it is not generally conscious of." The instinct presents specificity because each living being has his/her own instinct, which is specialized (i.e. closely adapted to one of the requirements of the life of the species). It is hereditary or innate, while also being spontaneously uniform with a comprehensively indecomposable structure.

CHAPTER 10:

THE HABIT

To organize our action and to facilitate our tasks, mankind will acquire habits. According to Paul Ricoeur, a French philosopher best known for combining phenomenological description with hermeneutics, habit refers to a way of acting, feeling, thinking, and perceiving, which are primarily acquired and relatively stable. A habit is, therefore, a general disposition with respect to all stimulants of the same species, and it is relatively permanent. A habit is a stable state, which constitutes a second nature and no habit is actually quite passive. This acquired reactivity, helps the individual tolerate certain impressions or accomplish certain acts without trouble or effort with a greater facility than in the past.

Classifications of Habits

There are eight different types of habits.

From the point of view of their content we can distinguish:

1. **Organic habits:** These involve habituation to a climate, to high altitudes, to a certain mode of nourishment, and more. For example, when our eyes become accustomed to light or darkness.

2. **Motor habits:** The body does primarily play an imperative role,

but sometimes the mind intervenes in varying degrees. The habit, for example, as in the tics people develop is at times, acquired mechanically and independently of the will. Correspondingly, familiar gestures sometimes require an apprenticeship, as in the examples of learning to type on a keyboard or drive a car.

3. **Mental habits:** These are habits of intelligence; for instance the habit of applying the rules of spelling when writing or problem-solving when doing mathematics.

4. **Habits of the heart:** These refer to the habits of allowing the self to being moved easily or mastering one's feelings.

5. **Habits of the will:** These involve knowing to make a decision or to hesitate.

6. **Moral habits:** These entail the habits of being fair, for example, using a respectful way of communication or speech.

7. **Social habits:** These include professional habits and the ways for acting in public, i.e. social situations.

8. **Artistic habits:** These include artful habits, such as playing a new piece of music at the piano.

There is also a distinction between passive habits and active habits.

In the passive habit, the subject would be limited to experience an impression to which he/she becomes less and less sensitive, with passage of time. For example, the perfume factory worker who, in time, no longer able to distinctly smells odors.

In the active habit, the mind and the will intervene, causing the individual perception to become more distinct and the movement easier and more prompt.

Habits and Instincts

By definition, habit is opposed to instinct. The instinct presents itself as an innate know-how while the habit presents the mandatory attribute of being acquired. But, once acquired, the habit entails certain characteristics of instinct, i.e. involuntary, subconscious, blind, and specialized.

Involuntary: If acquiring the habit requires some voluntary effort, this acquired habit will proceed smoothly and effortlessly, as in the habits of writing, dancing, etc.

Subconscious: If the habit takes place automatically without requiring the continuous control of consciousness, it develops as a subconscious habit. An example is the cyclist who pedals subconsciously.

Blind: We sometimes automatically perform usual acts that do not meet the need of our action, thus rendering our conduct blind. For example, having to lace my shoes, I will foolishly start wearing my watch.

Specialized: This habit is strictly specialized in hundreds of domains. For example, if I usually have the habit to type on a keyboard, it does not imply that I can also play the piano; as both require conditioned finger behaviorism.

The Formation of Habit

The mechanistic findings for habit and reflex explained the acquisition of the habit by an association and a chain of small reflex movement. Thus, a habit would be reduced to a chain of disengaged reflexes. At the onset, an act is analyzed into a simple element that gets repeated and finally comes to associate it with the next act. Take dancing, for example. The simple movements – 1 step, 2 steps, 3 steps, 4 steps – signals the following dance step.

The association between the signal and the reaction would also depend on a law called the "law of effect," which constitutes the principle of behavior conditioning. For example, in the experiment of inserting a white rat in a T- shaped labyrinth, the rat is allowed to go either of the two ways: Down the path that has food or down the path that holds an electrifying grid. Through repeated trials, we will see the rat will eventually get into the habit of always heading towards the food (pleasure).

The Mechanistic Findings

(The Gestaltism)

Gestaltism tries to understand the laws and conditions underpinning the ability to acquire meaningful perceptions, in a world that appears chaotic. From an experiment, conducted for a subject, to learn how to type, Paul Guillaume a French psychologist, observed that the final movement is never a juxtaposition of the old movements as explained by the mechanistic theory. Instead, it is rather a reorganization, which eliminates unnecessary movements. For example, while typing an essay today, my typing of this essay does not present a backward reference, as it is a new essay, nor does it indicates to my good skills of typing. Because acquiring a typing skill does not mean that I can just type one style of text, but I can type a variety of texts. Thus, the acquired habit involves not just the association but also the reorganization of elementary movements.

How Do we Acquire Habits?

Several factors impact the formation of habits, starting with the repetition of the act, although repetition singularly is not enough to form a habit. Jost's Law (in 1897), called the law of the optimum spacing of exercises, affirms that it is necessary to distance the repetitions according to an optimum interval for which the number of repetitions is smaller. This is because all acquired progress mandates a certain maturation before accomplishment of further progress.

However, as regards development of useful habits, repetitions, even if spaced, would not be enough. You have to graduate the difficulties of each level. We must therefore decompose the act into elementary gestures, not simply because they are easier, but to leave the old automatisms and substitute them for the new automatisms.

Correspondingly, even though, it would be necessary to associate, the effective manifestation of this association differs. According to the Mechanists, it is conducted in a completely mechanical manner via the trials and errors process, wherein particularly, the errors are eliminated. The Gestaltists criticized these findings. Correspondingly, according to Paul Guillaume, the act in the repetition is modified because the organization of the perception has been modified.

Learning thus corresponds to the acquisition of a "schema," (i.e. of the overall appearance of the form), which results in the orientation of the subject towards his/her activity. It is therefore not a question of a sum of determined movements, which repetition would have associated, but of an overall structure that constitutes a whole – or a form.

In addition, the structures are not ready-made and immutable, and rather built bit by bit during learning. They are capable of being modified to apply to particular cases, which is why Burloud said that "the schema of a habit is transposable and plurivalent."

The Psychic Functions Involved
in the Acquisition of a Habit

It is obvious that no learning can succeed in absence of some emotional motivations (i.e. tendencies).

Intelligence, to a certain extent, intervenes in the superior animals, and is more evident in mankind. Intelligence substitutes to a blind acquisition, or a more or less immediate understanding. Also, the mechanical memory is always accompanied by some logic, such as the way of representing a certain task, the comparison of the results with the target that are aimed at, the mental attitude at the time of acquisition and during the period of maturation, for example, the measurement of progress, etc.

Finally, let us add the will to learn, our attention and our effort to practice activities as well as exercise our being.

Metaphysical Meaning of Habit:
Habit and Inertia

The materialistic findings reduced habit to the inertia of the body, and to the functioning of the nervous impulse. Inertia is a property of matter, with the function to always persevere it in a static state. Habit is therefore easy due to the neurons frayed by a large number of passages of the nerve impulses. Habit, then, would constitute a property of matter of the body; it is a bend acquired by the body. This materialistic perspective reduces habit to inertia, and this is unacceptable. Habit results from the adaptive activity of the organism that can never be compared to inert matter.

Maine de Biran, a French philosopher, has criticized the materialistic perspectives. He distinguished between active habits which, to be acquired, require the intervention of intelligence and also of will. Therefore, meaning cannot be reduced to the inertia and passive habituation, which represent the outcome states and are explained by the theory of inertia. For example, the habit of walking barefoot, or accustoming oneself to a certain climate.

Correspondingly, extensive discussion has surrounded the findings by Maine de Biran about habit because none of the habits can be termed completely passive. Félix Ravaisson Mollien, a French philosopher, stated that even in habituation, "it is always a living being that adapts to its environment." Habit, therefore, bears the mark of life and the mind.

However, habit also presents a paradoxical nature. Particularly it is evident in the case of an intelligent individual, who sometimes invests a great effort to acquire certain habits. **However, once constituted, the very same habits become automated no longer present apparent characteristics of intelligence and of life.** However, notably, this must not lead us to discern that the will and liberty comprise the basis of habits.

Habit, Freedom and Nature

All will and all ideas followed by a certain number of exercises materialize in movements. Consider a novice dancer, who develops flawless, spontaneous, and instinctive dance movements with intelligence and a great effort of rehearsals of the necessary steps.

The automation of habit therefore constitutes the essential intervention of a non-mechanical being. Thanks to habit, the idea becomes expressive through the body via natural will and presents the spontaneity of the involuntary act.

In habit, the body ceases to be the enemy of the soul. Considering the same example, at the beginning of the dancing lessons, the body of the novice dancer would resist the errors due to awkwardness. And, only when, the habit of dancing is skillfully acquired that his/her body ceases to be an obstacle. In fact, the body then becomes an interpreter, an expression of the idea. The body, says Hegel, "is here taken over by the soul, thus it becomes its instrument." That is why we agree with Félix Ravaisson Mollien that habit is the meeting point of the mind and body. In a habit, the body is no longer foreign to the individual, but the individual is the body. The habit is the means through which the individual will is expressed. Therefore, a habit is the necessary mediation and the realization of an individual's projects and is the meeting point of the mind (thoughts) and matter.

Correspondingly, a habit, which is a mean of incarnation of freedom, sometimes imprisons this freedom and the human being becomes like a body with an abandoned soul. This shows us the ambivalence (positive and negative aspects) of the habit, which has advantages and disadvantages.

Advantages of the Habit

At the level of an action, the habit is not always strictly specialized and can at times be transposed to other domains. In such a scenario, it constitutes a rather general scheme, which can be transposed to a multiplicity of similar tasks. For example, a good driver can easily drive any car.

In an analogous way, the number of habits anchored in the human being, is found to be exactly proportional to the flexibility in conduct. The taxi-service driver, for example, due to the nature of the job, can more easily avoid an accident than the average driver.

Another benefit is that an individual who acquired habits can easily improvise and subsequently, when desired create the appropriate solution to an unexpected situation. Thus, habits allow us to invent more easily. For example, an experienced speaker can easily improvise a speech.

Finally, a habit as affirmed by Mounier is, "an instrument of the creative activity," because it can constitute a capital, which we can draw from, projecting the need to deepen our research, create, and invent.

Disadvantages of the Habit

According to the Swiss philosopher Jean-Jacques Rousseau, **"the only habit that must be given to the child is to contract none."** In what sense can Rousseau be justified? The answer is when habit loses its suppleness and its plasticity and it replaces the schemes by stereotypes.

In addition, Mounier stated that habit is like a sick man approaching a spiritual death. Correspondingly, the habit mechanizes the life of the individual and makes us prisoner of a routine.

At the level of affectivity, we notice that habits dull our feelings. For example, the repetitive sight of misery will harden one's heart.

Similarly, at the intellectual level, as corroborated by Gaston Bachelard, a French philosopher, the habit constitutes an epistemological obstacle preventing the human being from realizing the truth. An individual risk, in this case, is the likelihood of being interested in reading and listening to the ideas to which the individual is accustomed. Therefore, this individual will lose all critical thinking with regard to the concepts considered irritating. Habit also, on becoming routine, prevents openness to others, and different cultures and lock us in habitual intellectual concepts (i.e. always the same ideas without experiencing any innovation). It is in the corresponding sense that Nietzsche compared a habitual individual to a eunuch of knowledge (someone who loses knowledge). This has made certain people say that scientists were useful to science in the first half of their lives and useless in the other.

Furthermore, habits often create problems, consequently forcing us to act ineffectively, however to free oneself of them is difficult. This can be attributed to the fact that they are the illusion of comfort. Habit can also prevent maturation and enrichment of our emotional life, perhaps by imprisoning it in its infantile old forms. In this regard, psychoanalysis has clearly evidenced the danger of the habit, which may be at the source of neuroses. For example, the feeling of metamorphosis entails a transfer as a form of affective habits, i.e. a generalized timidity sourcing from fear of the father. This shyness manifests itself as an archetype related to all what is hidden in the subconscious of that individual from feeling of parental fear and where timidity reveal itself as a substitute of such fear.

As a routine, habit can also freeze art, morals, religion and language. To establish beauty, the painter must cover the canvas; to bring about justice the lawyer must consult the written law; and to specify the revelation the church must resort to dogmas. Similarly, to express an idea, an individual resorts to the mediation of the language. **However, it can be safely inferred that artistic works, the laws of morality, and the dogmas of religion and language are all works of the mind.**

Nevertheless, these masterpieces can sometimes find themselves in contradiction with the mind, when they imprison it in the too-tight knits of habit. Indeed, the literal application of the law can lead to a great injustice. Dogmas have been likewise, known to threaten to freeze the church and religion. Similarly, language may also present perils, such as falling into verbalism.

Habits give the mind a body, but sometimes the body is transformed into automatisms and forgets the imperative function to embody the mind. Habit must remain a faithful servant of the spirit, an intermediary between it and the body. It must not cover the risk of becoming foreign to it, or it may result in the alienation of the mind.

Mankind easily believes that with which he/she has been familiar with for a long time and correspondingly, anything new brings forth apprehension. The old and accustomed seem, to our nature, something that has always proven itself through experience, notably though herein the habits exhibit an oppressive nature.

The individual who, by a voluntary effort, has acquired a habit can, by will, control his/her habits and can free himself/ herself from them when they become oppressive.

CHAPTER 11:

ATTENTIVE CONSCIOUSNESS OR ATTENTION

Attention is a very general function of the psychic life, pertaining to the concentrations of consciousness on a certain object. For example, while reading a text objectively, an individual strives to develop a clear awareness and consciousness of the contained ideas. To pay attention, therefore, to an external object is also to observe and to pay attention to an interior object, to an idea or thought. Thus, attention is nothing, but thinking.

Attention is not a separate faculty but a combination of all the intellectual functions of the mind and the body, working in tandem with the objective of discovering what is real. Any type of attention involves a form of distraction. For example, I am distracted from anything that is not a defined object of the focus of my current attention. In conjunction, this distraction is absolute. For example, we are in state of reverie, we do not fix our thoughts on any determined object but we let them wander from one place to another. **Attention is thus characterized by the presence of a privileged object in the fields of my consciousness. This privileged object is chosen by the attentive mind, where the mind is passive and the object imposes itself on my consciousness.**

The Forms of Attention

1. Spontaneous attention, passive or involuntary, and mechanically automatic: It is done without any effort from our consciousness. It obeys the law of the interest and the selected activity by the mind. It does not depend on my will but on my desires, on my tastes, on my tendencies, and on my daily habits. We can sometimes pay attention to a certain object despite ourselves, which is dependent on the intensity, the suddenness or the strangeness of that object.

2. The deliberate reflective or intellectual attention: **This form of attention is the "real" attention.** It presupposes effort, constraint, and training on the part of an individual and his/her motivations. This is exemplified in our efforts to avoid a conversation and direct our attention towards fulfilling a duty.

The Nature of Attention: Attention and Fascination by an Object

The Empiricist Perspectives (Condillac, etc.)

Notably, it is not consciousness that accords attention but the object that imposes itself on our consciousness. All attention is somewhat passive, as it is a simple yet dominant and exclusive sensation, whose cause is in the intensity of the impression of the external object imposition on us. A sensation becomes attention either because it is alone or because it is more vivid compared to all others. Therefore, to be attentive implies being fascinated by the object and to be captivatingly drawn to it.

These findings highlight a purely passive phenomenon, wherein the attention supposes the effort, dynamism, activity, and the selection. For example, while on the train, I can refrain from hearing the crowds in the corridors and the noises of tracks to listen to the murmuring words of my neighbor.

In addition, the experimental psychology has highlighted this possibility of attention, wherein it resists disturbing factors. In their experiments, the scholars submitted two groups of student to a test: both groups had a task to cross all the "Ts" of a multi-page text. While, one of the groups worked in a silent classroom, the other worked in a class filled with noise. According to the study results both the groups provided an equally satisfactory job. This experiment, thus demonstrates that attention projects the power to resist external stimuli, which is outside of the chosen object of focus and towards which we direct our consciousness.

On the other hand, it is not the intensity of the stimulus that creates attention; it is the attention that makes the intensity of the stimulus. For example, if the different personalities of a painter, a hunter, and two lovers are in the same forest, each one of them will accord distinct attention to the exact same landscape, based on their tendencies and interests. Specifically, the painter will focus on colors, the hunter on the presence of animals, and the lovers on the romantic atmosphere. Therefore, in order to understand attention, one cannot ignore the interests and tendencies of the attentive person.

The Gestalt Perspectives (Kurt Koffka, Max Wertheimer, Wolfgang Köhler).

According to the Gestalists, as I open my eyes to the world, I look at certain objects that stand out owing to particular shapes that impose themselves on me. While concurrently, the landscape remains as a simple background of no significance. Thus, the best form in our vision field is imposed on us. The process is used in advertising techniques, which, thanks to characteristic and objective processes, unite our attention, adjust our field perspective, and then keep it alive by engaging us in a deeper way.

The objective value of the object is certainly significant as regards spontaneous attention, however the subjective value accorded to the subject (a person) needs to be considered concurrently. Alternatively, the form of the object fascinates us and the fascination is the opposite of the attention, because the attentive consciousness is rather vigilant.

Attention and Dynamism of the Person

Attention implies both an expectation and a tension (to stay put or wait) from the person. It is an expectation, which implies that to pay attention to an object, one must be notified, and to wait to meet it. William James, in alignment, gives the example of a young man who, while in his room located next to his father's office, awaits a signal from his friend of his presence in the garden by throwing small rocks at his window. When the rock strikes the window, only the young man pays attention while the father continues to read his newspaper peacefully. Evidently, the father did not hear anything because he did not expect anything. Exercising a careful attribute is therefore, an anticipation of an upcoming event, which employs our memories and all our mental resources to host this event. The more one is informed about a subject, the more attention he/she pays to it.

However, the tension (to stay put or wait) can be dispersed, as in the example of the student who waits attentively to receive the paper to get the subject of the exam. This student has mobilized all his/her mental resources, however as this psychic energy fails to finds any point of support, it diffuses into emotional reactions. But, in the instant when the supervisor distributes the papers with the subject, this restlessness calms down. Hence, the latent dispersion follows the mental tension and consequently this tension is consciousness brought to its highest degree. It is essentially an activity of selection, discernment, and synthesis.

Thus, this raise is the question: Which is the attentive part of the person - the body, or the mind? (Attention is a psychophysiological activity). If attention is the concentration of consciousness brought to a highest degree, is it then only a mental activity?

The Ribot perspectives discussed how he reduced attention to a biological function serving the interests of the living being and his/ her needs. Similarly, Ribot added that attention is reduced to motor phenomena.

Is attention a biological function? Attention is an automatic reaction of interests, and it is never voluntary but always spontaneous. Thus, for example, when I pay attention to the lecture of the teacher, what I am interested in may not be the lecture itself. I probably would be interested in getting a good grade, succeeding on the upcoming exams, or in avoiding a school punishment.

Is attention reduced to motor phenomena? Correspondingly, interest leads to the motor phenomenon of attention, alerting the body (such as fixing the eyes in a certain direction or towards a specific object, etc.). Thus, in absence of the intervention of central nervous system, attention refers to an organic reaction aroused spontaneously by an interest. It is, therefore, an attitude of the body.

Critical Reflection on Attention Perspectives

We cannot avoid admitting the physical behavior of attention. A mental attitude of attention is unimaginable without an attitude or a physical tension, analogous to how one cannot affirm the existence of unmotivated, disinterested, voluntary act. **We know that there is no unmotivated act, as motivation can be direct or indirect, apparent or hidden, conscious or subconscious, and thoughtful or instinctive.**

Moreover, we cannot admit or conform the assertion of Ribot, that attention is only a physical reaction. How, then, can we explain that an individual can look without seeing or hear without listening, if we do not admit that there is an attitude of tension of consciousness, in addition to the physical attitude?

In fact, with a tired consciousness, post a long concentration period, I can continue to fix my eyes towards the object of interest, without noticing much of what it in my vision field, and hear without actually listening. It is important to note that perception is always channeled by our current fixation.

Similarly, it is unacceptable to reduce all attention as being spontaneous. Between the spontaneous attention to an explosion in proximity and the voluntary unmotivated attention sustained despite fatigue and the desire to sleep, there is a difference that cannot be neglected. The spontaneous attention belongs to a dispersed personality and the voluntary attention belongs to a unified personality. Voluntary attention is the very expression of this power of mental synthesis, and often the former is confused for the latter. **Additionally, we can conclude that attention presents a psychophysiological phenomenon; a physical and mental tension. It is a reaction of interest, sometimes spontaneous, and sometimes voluntary.**

CHAPTER 12:

PERCEPTION AND SENSATION

From the Felt Quality
to the Perceived Object

Perception presents the Empiricist knowledge of the external world. This perception is underpinned by the sensation, without the knowledge or awareness of what is immediately experienced by a person. **Our real experience of the world is not that of sensation but rather of perception… because we do not grasp pure sensations but we perceive objects, qualities, and values.**

Correspondingly, only pure sensation can be attained in experiments at laboratories. For example, an esthesiometer limits the provision to compare the luminous intensity of two colored plates using human vision. In another example, as regards of some pathological case like tactile agnosia, patients are unable to recognize an object through touch. Therefore, the most common response to them touching a pen cap would be, "It's cold and it's smooth," but they will be incapable of interpreting sensory impressions. Such patients are restricted in their capacity to perceive, as perception here is primarily reduced to sensations.

Nature of the Sensation

Sensation is a biological reaction of the sensory organ to its environment and depends on the organs much more than the stimulant. For example, the same mechanical stimulant by different organs provides different reactions. Correspondingly, mechanical excitation of the acoustic nerve, leads to hearing of noise, yet if we use the same mechanical stimulant for the optic nerve, it would cause visions.

However, different types of stimuli applied on the same nerve elicit analogous reactions. For example, the optic nerve gives similar reactions to a luminous stimulant, which gives eyes a visual sensation, and a mechanical stimulus applied to the eye also gives a luminous impression.

Therefore, the sensation cannot be termed as a copy of the stimulant but in fact, it is a synthesis. When we see a red light, we do not see the four hundred trillion isolated vibrations, but we synthesize it in a strict timing to perceive the color red. The sensory organs fail to grasp the full range of vibrations that exist in nature. Instead, they make a selection. Sensation retains from its environment singularly the objects of interest to the living being in an effort to adapt.

The Law of Weber

Humans present a very limited sense of the surrounding world, because our senses (vision, hearing, touch, smell and taste) disregard almost all the virtually infinite amount of information around us. Thereby, allowing us access to a very narrow band of available information.

Our five senses, in fact, are the tentacles of our own ego and do not capture all the scales of existence. Evidently, there is a certain threshold, inside of which we can only capture some sensation. Due to these limitations, our perception of reality is very subjective. **Why is this so?**

Vision

The human vision cannot capture infrared and ultraviolet colors, nor can we see up to an endless point, as then things start to appear smaller, i.e. the further away they are from us. As well, we need optimally bright light to be able to see. Have you ever noticed when a ray of sunshine comes through the window, you can suddenly see all the tiny particles of dust that appear in the air (when you could not see them without the light being reflected onto them?) This variability of vision, is also evidenced in the case of nocturnal animals. These animals do not need much light to see in the dark and, while opposite to us, they are not able to see in sunlight.

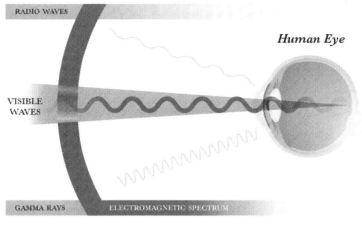

#2 : THE HUMAN EYE AND THE VISIBLE WAVES

Let us now demonstrate, with the following example, how our perception or vision may be narrow and selective.

Observe the table below. All the dots are white, aren't they?

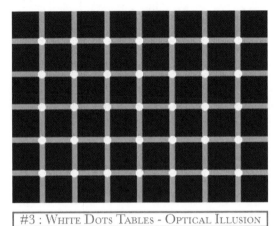

But as I move my eyes across the image, they appear to blink between black and white. This is an optical illusion, whereby the light frequency actually doesn't change. However, the preconscious processing of this image by my brain undergoes alteration.

Can you see, what is wrong with the Margaret Thatcher images provided below? Obviously, we notice that the images of the two faces are upside down, but can you notice that there is something a little bit odd about one of them? It has been observed that majority of people are able to identify and state the difference between the two; however, the problem is not immediately evident.

On the previous image, Margaret Thatcher's eyes and mouth are inverted. Although, despite such significant alteration, it's not that easy to see. And to the extent that if you briefly look at the images, without prior notice to the fact that they have been alterations to one of them, most people won't notice the change at all. However, when we look at the below images in the right orientation, the difference then is very apparent and even quiet terrifying.

The Thatcher illusion was reported first by Professor Thomson at the University of York in the year 1980. This optical illusion is operative not only on the Thatcher face but on any other face, when similarly modified.

It is, therefore, obvious that an individual's vision can be easily fooled. Not only can we see black dots where there are none, but oftentimes we can look at something and draw an interpretation, which may on viewing it from a different angle, appear as a total misinterpretation.

These images are confusing. If we assume that what we saw is what is "really out there," then we are in for a big surprise. This is because what we see is in fact, a pattern that is just in our minds.

Hearing

Hearing works by funneling sound along the ear canal, and when these sound waves hit our eardrums they cause sound vibrations, subsequently interpreted as sound by our brain. Humans present a limited range of hearing, i.e. between 20 Hz (Hertz) and 20 kHz (kilohertz). Everything before and after our eardrum does not notify us of their occurrences. However, a high-pitched wavelength would cause pain and even injury to the human or animal ear. At a young age, the ears present the ability to hear a wider range of sounds, which diminishes with age.

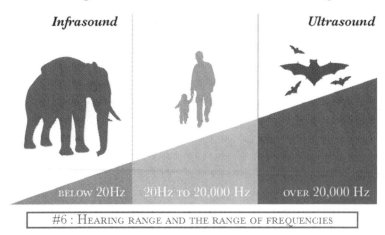

Infrasound   *Ultrasound*

BELOW 20Hz   20Hz TO 20,000 Hz   OVER 20,000 Hz

#6 : HEARING RANGE AND THE RANGE OF FREQUENCIES

Touch

Touch does not seem to have a single sensory organ. Our skin is, indeed, most known as being receptive for the touch, however usually this perception involves a movement. Notably, the skin itself is not sensory and in fact, it contains several sensory systems. For example, itch, pain, ticklish, hot, cold, soft, rough, etc. Correspondingly, isolating touch, based on physiological and functional grounds has proven to be very difficult. We can conclude that touch is a compilation of multiple sensory modalities, since it involves a collection of distinct informational channels. However, touch sensorial organs presents their limits as well. When great pressure is applied, it may damage the sensors in our skin and create a permanent injury. As regards the sensitivity of touch in the animal world, literature review evidences the lack of any prominent studies.

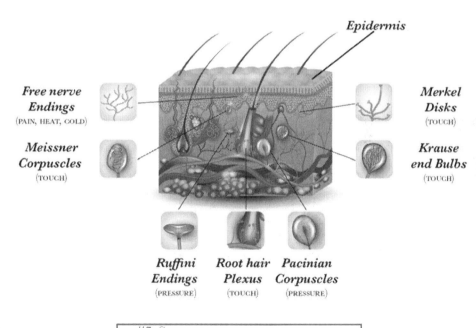

Epidermis

Free nerve Endings
(PAIN, HEAT, COLD)

Meissner Corpuscles
(TOUCH)

Merkel Disks
(TOUCH)

Krause end Bulbs
(TOUCH)

Ruffini Endings
(PRESSURE)

Root hair Plexus
(TOUCH)

Pacinian Corpuscles
(PRESSURE)

#7: SENSORY RECEPTORS IN HUMAN SKIN

Smell or Olfactory

According to science, the human nose can detect up to 1 trillion odors, allowing the organisms – which are composed of 50 million receptor cells – to identify the odorants of food, potential mating partners, dangers, and enemies. However, compared to other species, our olfactory bulb is considerably smaller, for example, it is smaller than that of a dog. This means that their sense of smell is comparatively stronger than ours and they can pick up the smells or odors of all sorts of invisible things. Correspondingly, a smell can register as a recognition sensation in our minds for several years and a disorder in smell can impact taste.

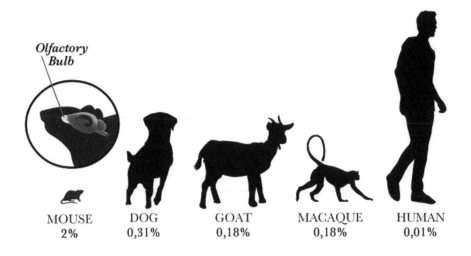

| MOUSE | DOG | GOAT | MACAQUE | HUMAN |
| 2% | 0,31% | 0,18% | 0,18% | 0,01% |

#8: PERCENT OF OLFACTORY BULB TO TOTAL BRAIN VOLUME

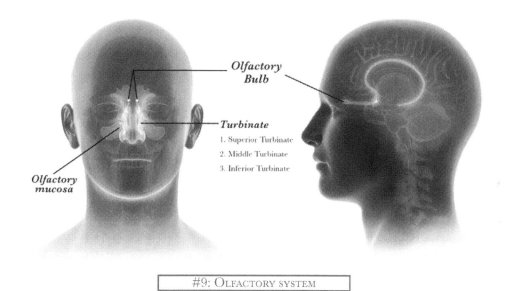

Olfactory
Bulb

Turbinate
1. Superior Turbinate
2. Middle Turbinate
3. Inferior Turbinate

Olfactory
mucosa

#9: OLFACTORY SYSTEM

Taste

We receive tastes through the sensory organs called taste buds, or gustatory calyculi, concentrated on the upper surface of the tongue. Our taste sensitivity is known to vary across different locations on the tongue and oropharyngeal cavity. A certain taste can be retained as a memory in our brain even after several years of sampling certain flavors. There are five basic documented tastes: sweet, bitter, sour, salty, and savories, often known by its Japanese term "umami." There are other tastes, such as calcium and free fatty acids, and likewise, science also indicates the existence of other basic tastes.

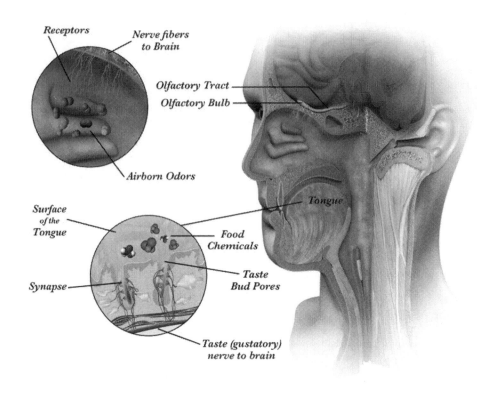

Receptors

Nerve fibers
to Brain

Olfactory Tract

Olfactory Bulb

Airborn Odors

Surface
of the
Tongue

Tongue

Food
Chemicals

Taste
Bud Pores

Synapse

Taste (gustatory)
nerve to brain

#10: Mouth Anatomy : The Sense of Taste

It is important to note that mankind seems to have a sixth sense, although it is not yet commonly acknowledged nor well understood, which consequently demonstrates our limited progress in the non-physical fields. The other relevant problem is the lack of knowledge amongst scientists as regards of the origin and source of this form of energy and sense.

Multisensory Integration

All of our senses follow the sensory processing process that organizes sensation from our bodies. Specifically, they deal with how the brain processes multiple sensory modality inputs, such as proprioception, vision, auditory system, tactile, olfactory, vestibular system, and taste into usable functional outputs.

Multisensory integration is vital for largely every activity performed by our body, because the combination of our multiple sensory inputs is essential to facilitate our comprehension of the surroundings and ourselves.

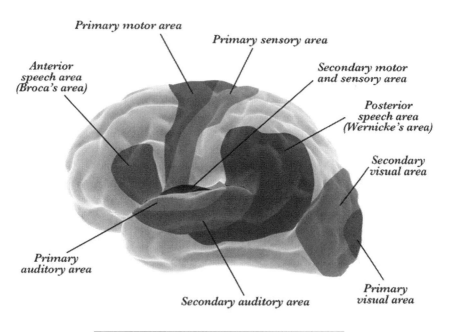

Primary motor area

Primary sensory area

Anterior speech area (Broca's area)

Secondary motor and sensory area

Posterior speech area (Wernicke's area)

Secondary visual area

Primary auditory area

Secondary auditory area

Primary visual area

#11: Brain Areas and their Functions

Correspondingly, my sensory experience is apparent as an unbiased mirror reflecting an external reality. Although my senses only detect a tiny part of this reality, although, even that may be extensive for my consciousness to handle. Moreover, our senses are limited by their threshold and by the bandwidth of information they provide. Thus, this, in turn, limits our perception of the world.

The preconscious brain edits the sensory experiences prior to their presentation to our consciousness. The mind can be compared to a subconscious editor, with the job to sort together the movie scenes of our life. It edits by neglecting some parts and adding others. Thus this function is underpinned by its underlying purpose to nudge us towards exposing what is subconscious to consciousness. This particular concept has been explored later on in the book.

The fact that we are unable to see, smell, hear, or even sense several things in the world make us certainly wonder. Correspondingly, cases of heightened or extra-sensory perceptivity experience across the five or six senses have been evidenced in certain people. However, this phenomenon has not yet been explored or documented by science. Those people may also perceive the word differently than the average human. Additionally, a person deprived of a sense, for example, a blind individual's perception of the world may very different from others with the gift of sight.

Plato, a Greek philosopher, in 427 BC, discussed that senses can only give you information about the ever-changing and imperfect world of phenomena, which are appearances, i.e. things as they seem to our senses and are associated with matter, time, and space. Therefore, they can only provide implications about an ultimate reality and not reality itself. However, on utilizing the reason, which goes straight to thought, we intuitively recognize the truth.

The Law of Fechner

As explored previously, there is a threshold relative to each sensation. Fechner's work showcased the growth of sensation as the logarithm of stimulant: Excitement grows in geometrical progression and sensation in arithmetic progression. Some of the most prominent perspectives on it are the Intellectualist perspectives.

Intellectualist perspectives have brought forward in depth discussion on the perception of the object in space, where sensation is subjective and qualitatively un-extended, and an object in space is extended. Therefore, how can we, from subjective data and an un-extended perception, conceive an extended object? Perceiving an object in space is an intellectual act (i.e. it is the reason that would yield, by a set of judgments, the sensible quality to that object).

Perception, therefore, refers to a set of transformed sensations, exteriorized and interpreted. For instance, we could say that in order to perceive a chair, I essentially must possess the sensation of certain lines and colors. These could be subsequently interpreted and organized to obtain the perception of this object (the chair).

It is therefore the intelligence, which, by a judgment would accord quality to the object. It is the intelligence, through its work of interpretation and synthesis, which essentially transforms sensations into perception, thereby giving sensations cohesion and meaning.

The Perception of Distance

Distance is never provided by sensation because it can never be something already assigned. It is not a sensory impression but is constructed and judged based on an interpretation of sensitive data, like the apparent size of objects and one's perspective of the objects. For example, I judge that an object is far away because I perceive it as being small, or that it is close because I perceive it as large. I still judge that a street goes really far because I see the edges despite the parallel sidelines meeting in the distance.

These interpretations are made through experience and memory. Specifically, the perception of distance is not innate but acquired and therefore requires some kind of learning. This attestation was advanced by George Berkeley, an Irish philosopher whose primary achievement was the advancement of a theory called "immaterialism," which was confirmed by the work of the surgeon William Cheselden.

Cheselden succeeded in operating on blind individuals who had congenital cataracts and restored their sight. The operated-upon subject declared at the outset that the objects touched his eyes, and only afterwards was he able to grasp the notion of distance. The role of judgment in the perception of space seems, again, to be highlighted by psychopathological data: Very often the disturbances of perception derive from disorders of the intelligence and of language. For example, patients suffering from language difficulties are also incapable of orienting themselves in space.

The Interpretation of Sensations: Perception of Significant Objects

Significant objects are never felt, and instead they are thought. It is the intelligence that recognizes them through experience, associations of ideas, and memories. Perception, subsequently, adds to the sensation, a complex tissue of memories, ideas, and judgments. For example, an individual can recognize a three-dimensional cube sitting on a table, attributed to a mental construction made from observation of the three faces and nine edges. This appearance of the three faces and the nine edges, reminds me the individual of an experience. Therefore, I remember, then I reason, and I subsequently conclude that the object is a cube. My perception is concurrently also dependent on my cultural background. For example, a bookshelf, according to my culture, is used for storing books. However, for others it simply refers to a wardrobe.

Illusions of the Senses Arise from Errors of Judgment

In our judgments, we project our knowledge and our memories. Thus, we may fail to perceive spelling errors while reading, and this is attributed to our projection of knowledge and memories on the reading of characters and words.

Can you read the below text?

"i cdnuolt blveiee taht I cluod aulaclty uesdnatnrd waht I was rdanieg. The phaonmneal pweor of the hmuan mnid, aoccdrnig to a rscheearch at Cmabrigde Uinervtisy, it dseno't mtaetr in waht oerdr the ltteres in a wrod are, the olny iproamtnt tihng is taht the frsit and lsat ltteer be in the rghi t pclae."

Only few people can. It says:

"I couldn't believe that I could actually understand what I was reading. The phenomenal power of the human mind, according to a research at Cambridge University, it doesn't matter in what order the letters in a word are, the only important thing is that the first and last letter be in the right place."

According to the Intellectualists, the sensation pertains to the state of elementary consciousness consecutive to an impression made on one of our sensory organs. Furthermore, the perception refers to the interpreted sensation that became meaningful to us (i.e. implying the notion of a certain external object to us, to be localized in space). This distinction between sensation, pure feeling, and perception, which is constructed by the mind, is no longer maintained by the modern psychology.

Modern Psychology (i.e. the school of the Gestaltism) has criticized the Intellectualist findings by deducing a lack of distinction between sensation and perception. And claims that by no means it can be demonstrated that sensation is at first subjective, requiring an intellectual work of objectification to become a perception. Similarly, the hypothesis of prior sensation is rejected because pure sensation as a lived experience does not exist. Perception is not a mental construct or a set of judgments. Correspondingly, the Gestaltists claim that Intellectualists have exaggerated the role of intelligence and mental constructs in perception.

The Gestaltist Findings

For Kurt Kofka and Wolfgang Köhler, two German psychologists, and Max Wertheimer, an Austro-Hungarian psychologist, perception is not a set of sensations but rather all perception is a perception of a whole. It is not intelligence that constructs a form with scattered sensations; instead, the form is felt or perceived from the start. For the Intellectualists, sensations are the matter of perception and it is judgment and memory that gives them a form. However, for Gestaltists, this distinction between sensation and perception does not exist today.

The form is inseparable from matter; it is given to us intuitively and matter constitutes its essence. Objects divide themselves without the intervention of the intelligence, simply by their own structure on an undifferentiated background. For example, I do not open my eyes on a world of objects, which are independent of my habits, my knowledge and my judgments but these objects are preexisting, organized and grouped according to the law of forms, i.e. as the simplest and the most coherent.

Perception of Distance

It is true that the perception of distance requires some learning. However, notably we present an immediate intuition of distance. We see that an object is far away not just because we observe that it is small but also because it is, indeed, at distance. Thus, perception of distance is an immediate intuition involving the maturation of cervical nerve connections. Distance is a natural structure of the perceived.

Gestalt Interpretation of the Illusion Perspectives

The illusion does not arise from the error of judgments, memories and knowledge, as is asserted by the Intellectualist perspectives, but rather from the overall structure of the object. This is similar to the example of the illusion offered by Franz Carl Müller-Lyer, a German sociologist. It consisted of arrows with diverging and converging chevrons (below image). During the experiment, when the participants were asked to place a mark at the midpoint of each arrow, they invariably placed it more towards the "tail" end. As the diverging chevron arrows projected the illusion to be longer compared to the converging ones, while in fact, both types of arrows have the exact same length.

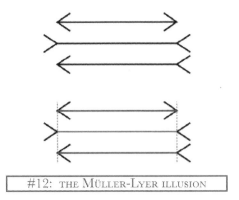

Critique of the Psychology of Forms

The phenomenology from Maurice Merleau-Ponty, a French phenomenological philosopher, was strongly influenced by the German philosophers Edmund Husserl and Martin Heidegger. It agreed with the Gestaltist views and the refutation of Intellectualism, stating that perception is not an association of judgments and reasoning. Perceiving is not reasoning.

Pure sensation does not exist. The totality of the perception takes control of the element. Therefore, perception is a spontaneous synthesis, original, and it progresses towards analysis. It is a relation of incarnate consciousness into the cosmos. However, the psychology of form accords significance only to the data and minimizes the role of the subject. It has been also studied that perception depends concurrently on the structure of the object and on the subject, on its habits, on its tendencies, and on its values.

Thus, perception can only be understood through the living being and its needs and its values. "I see the world as I am," said Paul Eluard, French poet and founder of the surrealist movement, "I do not see it as it is." Thus, the perceived world is full of ourselves but it is not the reflected intellectual self. Psychoanalysis has well emphasized the psychological role of the social in perception. For example, Swiss psychologist Hermann Rorschach's test demonstrates that, in our way of perceiving, there is a way of being that is projected.

The perceived world, which smiles with our own joy, or grimaces with our anguish, resembles our prejudices, is not, however, the objective world of science. In this perspective, the French philosopher Maurice Merleau-Ponty joined Henri Bergson, who had asserted that consciousness chooses in the external world what would respond to the need for its action.

Furthermore, regarding the perceptive illusions, they added that it is the situation of the body and the values privileged of the moment that regulate and decide the perception of movement in some well-known illusion. For example, the train I am on and the neighboring one appear in motion, even when either one starts to move. It must be observed that the illusion is not arbitrary and that I am provoking it at will by the all-intellectual choice and the attention from a point of reference.

Similarly, let's say if you were playing cards in your train compartment, you then would conclude that the other train has started to move. If, on the contrary, you are looking at someone in the neighboring train, it seems then that the occupied train has started to move. Each time it seems fixed to us one of the two objects that we have chosen to look at and became a reference point for us at that moment. Therefore, the global organization of the perceptual field is carried out by the subject-body in a situation.

The definition of perception would be that perception is a behavior of the living being, of those needs and of those values grappling with the universe.

Subjective Perception
and Objective Perception

Each of us grasps reality in a spontaneous and subjective way. The perception depends on its tendencies, needs, and interests. Each of us thus builds an intimate universe, or an "umwelt." For example, as mentioned earlier, the same forest will be interpreted differently according to the interest of the observer. The lover will find it beautiful, romantic, or as a refuge place. The botanist will perceive of it as a field for experiments.

Similarly, in our perception of the world, we do allow psychological projections. For example, we would say: The sky is grey and sad. Our perception of the world thus is influenced, as Bachelard tells us, by our subconscious desires.

To achieve the objectivity of perception, one must do the psychoanalysis of knowledge, and purify it from the subconscious desires underlying our affirmations. The objectivity of perception implies both necessity and universality.

CHAPTER 13:

<u>MEMORY</u>

The German philosopher Martin Heidegger said, "Mankind is the being of distant." And this is why we project the present on the future and confront the present with our perception of it. Mankind is able to find and fix the past, owing to the memory. He/she retrieves it again, but does not resuscitate it because the memory is not a hallucination. The individual simply reconstructs the past and thinks of it as the past.

Correspondingly, memory, according to the French philosopher André Lalande, is a psychic function, which consists of the reproduction of a past state of consciousness, with a character recognized as such by the subject.

The Fixing of Memories

Our memory does not fix all our perceptions and our experiences and makes a choice depending on two factors: the objective and the subjective.

Objective: The object, which is fixed in the memory is structured and presents the best form, according to the viewpoint of Gestaltism. For example, it would be easier for a memory to fix a harmonic melody as compared to a random sequence of some other kind of music.

Subjective: A memory is an act of a person that recollects the elements of our experiences, which are linked to our values, our tendencies, desires, requirements, worries, and others. A fixed memory may return to the mind either spontaneously or after a voluntary effort of evocation.

This discussion thus raises certain questions at this point: In what form does this fixed memory survive? How can it stay at our disposal? What happens to our memories when we do not think of them?

We will attempt to answer these questions now.

The Preservation of Memory: The Materialist Perspectives of Ribot (Memory and Habit)

According to Ribot, the memory is preserved in the brain in the form of material traces, capable of being awakened by present impressions. It presents a resemblance to the mechanism of the needle of an electrophone, which comes to awaken the music grained in the surface of the disc. Ribot's arguments, on which his views rest, are drawn from the anatomy-clinical considerations about certain diseases of memory, such as motor aphasia or the loss of memories of articular words. This is congruent to the Broca zone in the brain, which is responsible for apraxia or loss of memory of the gestures. It also shows a similar association to a connection of the psychomotor zones of the frontal lobe. The loss of a cerebral territory entails that of the corresponding memories.

Memory, according to Ribot, is thus a collection of visual images (tactile, articulatory, and graphic) deposited in cerebral territories to record the sudden impressions and to preserve the trace.

The views of Ribot, shared by Bergson, are confirmed by the present neurology.

The memory, as perceived by layman is not a print image in the brain that a lesion can remove. The destruction of a cerebral territory removes not the corresponding memories but only the possibility of their evocation under certain conditions. An aphasic, for example, is an individual, who does not present a memory loss of words but struggles to find them with a reactive or weak brain.

There is a possibility of regaining this ability to revoke such capacity as a result of an emotional shock. Dr. Jean Delay, a French psychiatrist and neurologist, states that a sick person incapable of making the sign of the cross spontaneously when entering a church, through re-education of the hemisphere which is not affected by a lesion. For example, an aphasic, who has lost memory of articulating words as a result of a binding in the left hemisphere of the brain, can regain remembrance while reeducating the right hemisphere.

Bergson's Distinction of Memory and Habit

According to Bergson, Ribot evidences confusion in his comprehension of memory and habit. Ribot thought he was discussing memory while he actually only spoke of habit; as it is the habit, in fact, and not memory, which is explained by neuromuscular connections, mounted in the organism by material traces preserved in the nervous tissue. Thus, reciting a poem learned by heart is a habit acquired after several repetitions and an overall organization. This recited poem is a habit, which is stored in a closed system of automatic process. Thus, in the habit, the past is resurrected, used, and not thought of as past.

True and pure memories are quite different from a habit. Habit will be acquired and be best registered in the brain by repetition, while a memory will not be registered by exercise. The act of reciting a poem from memory is a habit, but evoking the conditions in which this learning took place for the first time is an act of pure memory. Habits are mechanisms, whereas pure memories are singular images representing an instant of our history. **Thus, habit is passive while memory is active. Memory is an instantaneous actualization of the past.**

Bergson's Findings of Memory: Memory as an Intellectual Act

Memory is the mind or consciousness insofar as it lives and lasts, does not belong to matter, and consequently is independent of nervous mechanics. Remembrance is not preserved in matter, and because the mind is hard (and operates in a linear way, a continuity in time), nothing of what the mind has made is lost. Thus, not the preservation of memories but oblivion will cause then a problem.

Let's now talk about the problem of forgetting. **How is it that my entire past is not presently conscious for me?**

Bergson states that consciousness is a biological function, which evidences the purpose to adapt ourselves to the present action. Therefore, to act in the present, it would be useless to be aware of the totality of our past. Consciousness only illuminates memories, which are immediately useful to us. Herein, Bergson places significant projection to the role of the organism and especially on the brain. The brain does not serve to preserve the memories that are preserved in the subconscious. Instead, it serves to update the memories and to filter those, which are useful for the present action. The brain is in fact the guardian of memories, which operates as the instrument of their conscious evocations.

In dreams, memories are no longer selected and this could be attributed to the non-existent dimension of the demands of action. Attention to life is relaxed, and the images of the past that are relived then flood in abundance and in disorder.

The problems of memory disorders usually are associated with the excessive fatigue of the brain inducing a severely weakened mental state. Therefore, it would be difficult and sometimes even impossible to evoke memory. **But memory itself continues to exist in the subconscious.**

Bergson's findings present a detailed discussion of the preservation of the past and recognition of memories. This perspective is better than Ribot's, where the facts that are brought to light by the nervous pathology, but it presents a metaphysical difficulty. Bergson therefore considers memory as a pure consciousness, which could be optimally utilized to actualize memories by means of the brain.

Here is the problem that arises: How can memory, which is pure consciousness, be used for the actualization of memory, which is purely a material mechanism of the brain functions? A second problem also arises when considering this: What can we say about this integral conversation of the past in a purely psychic subconscious?

As stated by Ribot, memories, irrespective, they are considered as material imprints, or as mental images from Bergson. According to these two findings they are, indeed, preserved. In fact, our mind preserves things and traces. Therefore, according to Ribot and Bergson, memories are accounted to be things.

Alternatively, whether memory is a physiological material trace or a psychic trace, the difficulty remains the same. "A conserved perception is a perception, it continues to exist, it is always in the present, it does not open behind us that dimension of escape and absence, that is the past," said Maurice Merleau-Ponty.

What is Memory Really About?

The perspectives of Husserl and Merleau-Ponty claim that remembrance is not in consciousness. Rather, consciousness itself constitutes it, positioning the past as a past. Memory is not attributed as a thing but an act of consciousness. It is a judgment of the mind that reports certain events in the past. If memory is an act of consciousness, remembrance is the present act of evoking an event, relating it to the past. **It is a reconstruction of it from the present.**

However, something in the form of a memory trace needs to be conserved in order to allow the possibility for the evocation of the past. These "memory-assistants" are equally of an organic as well as a social nature. Our ability in recognizing a past event is based on social references (a date, a place, a major social event like Independence Day, natural disasters, war and others). This is because of these references that we are able to place our memories in the past. These markers constitute the social frameworks of our memory. Based on the guidelines we adopt, we can evoke the most diverse memories. An individual can present several memories sourcing from family, friends, professional, national, etc. Maurice Halbwachs, a French philosopher and sociologist, said "the past is not preserved, it is rebuilt from the present while recognizing it and positioning it as a past." We can agree with this, although it is also necessary to distinguish between sensorimotor memory, autistic memory, and social memory.

The sensorimotor memory, or motor-sensory memory, is equivalent to memory-habit or memory-action. Bergson refers to it as the habitual memory. In the habit, the individual recovers his/her past but does not conceive of it as past.

Autistic memory is made of personal singular images outsourced from the past, into the dream, however, notably this memory is not a true memory. In the dream, the images are not recognized as memories by our dream consciousness. The dreamer, like the individual of habit, relives the past, but does not conceive of it as past.

The social-memory and actual memory are linked to the demands or needs of the social group, and is a function of reason. Pradines wrote that memory is "a reconstruction of the past through the usage of intelligence." It is, as Pierre Janet acknowledged, "the conduct of narrative," as it consists of telling a past event.

The Problem of Memory Reliability

Memory is a present evocation of the past, but this evocation is not a simple and faithful replica of the past occurrence. It is a reconstruction – a rationalization of the past – and it presents itself with modifications dependent on the circumstances of the evocation. Thus the memory is presented simplified, impoverished, or enriched. For example, let us ask an individual to draw a sample of an architectural pattern. Then six months later, we invite this same person to redo the same drawing, however this time from memory. The very unfaithful memory of this act will undergo significant modifications and shall be schematized and intellectualized. The drawing made from memory will present regular shapes, rather more geometric than the initial model. Small dimensions will have been overestimated, large dimensions underestimated, and other details will have totally disappeared.

This is true also of our memories, which interest our values and present a connection with our tendencies that awaken in us an emotion at the moment of their evocation. However, these memories concurrently with evocation present themselves as impoverished and yet can appear enriched in another way. Remembrance is transfigured by all the events that succeed it, which will not fail to be reflected upon them on the occasion of future evocations.

Correspondingly, while Rousseau was writing his confession, he complacently evoked memories of his journeys on foot, his nights under the stars, and the adventures of his poor youth period. If Rousseau had remained his entire life adventure-less, for example, a vagabond would appear less poetic to him. The literary successes he had later in life contributed to his transformation and poetized the evocation of his adventurous youth.

The Perspectives of Affective Memory

Affective memory is the resurrection of feelings in the form of memories and is aroused by sensory stimuli, generally olfactory. For example, during a walk in the forest, the peculiar odor of dead leaves resuscitates in an individual the same feelings as felt during childhood.

The partisans of this type of memory believe in its absolute fidelity or loyalty. Marcel Proust, a French novelist, claimed that affective memory accidentally resurfaces in us the same emotions we experienced in the past. For example, by listening to the crackling of the fire in the chimney, Proust was seized by the memory of winters of his childhood as they were re-lived exactly with the same feelings as before.

Correspondingly, when several memories are evoked, they are accompanied by emotions. But are these aroused emotions really those that were experienced in the past?

Essentially, to speak of an affective memory such as these adaptations claim, it is imperative to be able to compare the emotion felt at present with corresponding emotion experienced in the past. In such a case, if the actual emotion is new or different, it is then permissible to doubt the presence of this memory. Eugène de la Croix, a French artist, said that when "the memories of an experienced aggression can provoke anger in me, we react violently to this memory but this anger is a present reaction, an emotion present itself rather way before than the memory of an emotion."

The integral resurrection of the past is a characteristic of habit and not of memory, for it is in habit that I am my past, although through memory I have a past. This so-called emotional memory supposes that it exists, and reduces itself to the habit of the conditioned reflexes. It is similar to Pavlov's dog experiment discussed in Chapter 1, where the dog salivated when hearing the sound of a bell, and regained the same emotion that aroused in the dog at the first stimulus (the meat).

Congruently, the same explanation can also be applied to the phenomenon of emotional transfer in psychoanalysis. The patient presents a recovery of his/her past, to regain the emotions and the very gestures of his/her childhood, but fails to remember them. The patient does not know how to relate his/her events to the past, because they do not realize that he/she reproduced past attitudes, so the memory is relived although it is not recognized.

Thus, it can be safely stated that if memory was really recognized, to return to the past, it would cease to be affective to become an intellectual act. Affective states are present in the order of the present. The memory is represented now but grafted as past. It would be better to speak then of a habit and not of an affective memory.

The Problem of Forgetting
and Memory Functions

It has been popularly said that memory is built to forget. Likewise, forgetting can only be understood from the individual perspective and not from an isolated function of the brain except in the cases of pathological brain lesions. Forgetting is evidently the converse of remembering.

The functions of memory:

1. The fixing.

2. The recall (spontaneous or voluntary).

3. The reconstruction of the past.

4. The recognition (a fundamental act of memory). Recognize which present event is on my mind and that it belongs to my past.

5. The localization; which is to date a recognized experience as belonging to the past. We refer to the benchmark event of collective life that social life offers us, such as a war, a trip, an accident, a party, etc.

6. Forgetfulness.

Memory requires the intervention of intelligence, in all its stages, except for forgetting, unless it is voluntary.

Forms of Forgetfulness

Abnormal or pathological forgetfulness is the radical impotence to evoke a memory. In extreme cases, it becomes a disease like amnesia. Where the brain is not able to retrieve the right path to evoke that memory.

Subconscious forgetfulness occurs when an individual who does not want to remember certain painful memories, ends up forgetting them. This phenomenon presents a variation and repressing that forgetfulness is unhealthy in some cases, while well-considered in other cases, for the balance of our personality.

Normal spontaneous forgetfulness is the operation of abstraction that makes us neglect certain aspects of beings and things in a selection dictated by the law of interest.

Normal rational forgetfulness is deliberate and exercised by will. It consists of an organization of knowledge, which further allows the mind to retain the essential and drop the superfluous. That is why it is said that knowing how to forget and knowing how to retain is an art of learning and cultivation.

The Causes of Forgetfulness: The Materialistic Perspectives (Ribot)

Normal forgetfulness is due to the erasure of the traces engraved in the brain, while pathological forgetfulness is sourced from the destruction or a lesion of the cerebral region in which it is located.

Memories cannot be studied as things. As discussed earlier, even in the pathological case, the brain lesion does not destroy the memory but only prevents it from being naturally evoked and thus, the patient can recover the lost word or gesture by means of an emotion. Consequently, as Bergson told us, the recall of memories is inseparable from the emotions of the person, from these affective conditions of the situation in which he/she finds himself/herself (similar to the previous example of the patient incapable of making naturally the sign of the cross, yet once he returns to the church he does it spontaneously).

Moreover, this human phenomenon, must be understood and not explained. It should be understood from the whole being because it reveals the person, his/her demands, and his/her worries.

Forgetfulness is significant, as indicated in Freud's psychoanalysis: "I do not forget anything except what is unbearable, painful or contrary to my demands." The forgetting of psychoanalysis can be attributed either to a lack of interest or due to repression. The first (lack of interest) pertains to a mean of defense of the self; the second entails pernicious because it causes complexes, and all that is repressed never dies. It is true that if these forgotten memories are expelled from the clear conscience of an individual, they continue to haunt, and can reappear in the form of morbid symptoms (similar to the previous example of the patient who, in his childhood, accidentally caused his brother to bleed and so always gets anxious when he sees red objects). This forgetfulness, as presented by psychoanalysis, depersonalizes and imbalances an individual, and there is a harmful omission in forgetting. There is another solitary forgetting, which is a sign of freedom.

According to Bergson, forgetting is a way of adapting to reality. Relatively, in order to better succeed in its present experience, the consciousness chooses from the past what is needed and which it is necessary for it to adapt. The human consciousness therefore presents an inclination towards the future, as it evokes to me the past in accordance with the assumed paths and the acts that it needs to accomplish.

Paramnesia (the Illusion of "Déjà Vu")

During instances of discovering a new landscape or listening to unknown music, we experience the feeling of having already seen this landscape or of having already heard this music. This feeling is called Paramnesia, or a "déjà vu," in French this literally means to have previously seen. Wherein, the present is given to us as if it were the past. This is what Dr. Jean Delay, a French psychiatrist called "the hallucination of the present, or the patient recovers the past as if he/she were present."

Explaining Paramnesia

According to Pierre Janet, this can be attributed to a simple tired nervous system and to a drop in psychological tension. In this scenario, a weakened, exhausted mind, incapable of responding to the demands of the present, spontaneously lives this present as in a dream as if it were a past.

For Bergson, in paramnesia, we dream of our life instead of living it, and the present events are given to us as if they have already happened, which is why we confuse the present with the past.

However, as evident from the discussion, neither the point of view of Janet nor that of Bergson really explained paramnesia, which is why we will have to refer back to Freud.

Freud endeavors to explain the specificity of the illusion of déjà vu. For example, one of his clients visited new friends and discovered their house for the first time, and surprisingly she experienced a striking impression of déjà vu. Here is the psychoanalytic explanation of the incidence: The client's friend had a seriously ill brother and also the client's brother was critically unwell, sometime back, and his sister subconsciously wished for his death. Thus, this memory is bound to a forbidden desire, which is evidently repressed. This subconscious desire surfaced and returned to consciousness, at the house. However, it was immediately transfigured and the impression of memory was projected on the house and its garden.

According to Freud, false recognition is a true recognition that is camouflaged in a false memory. It is the recognition of oneself subconsciously in a situation.

Can "Déjà Vu" be as Well a Glimpse Into a Past Life?

When it comes to discuss the concept of reincarnation, many people immediately reject this thought, and mainly this is due to their social conditioning. Nevertheless, there is a growing body of empirical evidence supporting the reality of reincarnation.

Conceivably, we can't absorb all of life lessons and which our souls are meant to learn, in just one singular lifetime. This fact is hard to ignore when we utilize our sensible thinking. There is a passage in the Quran where it states the following:

Surat "Al-Baqarah," which means "The Cow" (2:28): **"How can you disbelieve in Allah when you were lifeless and He brought you to life; then He will cause you to die, then He will bring you [back] to life, and then to Him you will be returned."**

Therefore, what would you understand when reading this text?

CHAPTER 14:

THE IMAGINATION

In common parlance, imagination is called the faculty possessed by the mind to create new things to escape from reality or the present. French philosopher Jean-Paul Sartre defined imagination as "the great unrealistic function of consciousness."

The problem of the imagination may, in fact, offer to be the most obscure problem. Psychologists clearly distinguish between what they have called the reproductive imagination and the creative imagination. The study of the first pertains more to the problem of memory. For example, in the case of a painter who reproduced from memory, a real landscape that he had already seen; in such scenario he used reproductive imagination. If, on the contrary, he painted on a canvas his inner vision of an imaginary landscape, he used his creative imagination.

Nature of the Imagination

The Empiricist perspectives have perceived consciousness as passive. The image is a reflection of the object and the reflection persists in consciousness. Thus, though the image has a mental quality; it has an organic material support, and therefore, it is, indeed a trace of the perception engraved in the brain. Hence, then, every image is the result of perceptions, i.e. reproductions of the object already perceived. David Hume, a Scottish philosopher, and Empiricist corroborated the same when he claimed that impressions are perceptions of the external world and our ideas, which are reflections or images of impressions in thought.

Imagination is, therefore, a weakened perception and the two concepts are primarily distinguished only by a simple difference of degree and intensity. Likewise, we can sometimes confuse certain cases of perceptions and imaginations, as in the following cases:

- In the waking state, we sometimes believe we have heard the sound of footsteps (which were actually a part of our dream).

- In the dream, we take for reality the mental images we see, which is why we sometimes say, "My dream was so real!."

- In a hallucination, one believes actually being able to see non-existent objects.

According to the Empiricist perspectives, only reproductive imagination is the existential form of imagination, creative imagination does not exist, and every image is sourced from perception. These scholars evidence the lack of imagery of colors amongst the blind and the lack of brain images (mental traces) of sounds amongst the congenital deaf as proof of their argument.

The Empiricist perspective is thus, well accounted as regards the nocturnal imagination (dreams, hallucinations) but fails to justify the imagination in the awakened state. In the dream, we often consider images to be reality; and the same is applied to hallucinations. For example, take the case of a person blinded due to a tumor. He does not know that he/she is blind because the tumor stimulates the cortical visual centers to release visual images. These, in turn, cause the patient hallucinations (i.e. such patient would believe that he/she is witnessing a fire although that may not be the current reality).

However, in the normal waking state, we are clearly able to distinguish between perception and images. For example, a person will never confuse an imaginary explosion with a low noise that he/she heard and perceived, irrespective the power of this imagination.

Sometimes we believe that someone is knocking at the door, but fail to find anyone at the door. We are sure that we heard a sound, and thus confusion ensues. **In this case, the perceived sound is real, we heard a noise, but the interpretation of that sound is false.**

Therefore, we are able to immediately distinguish in the conscious state between perception and an image. Hence, we can no longer admit that the only distinguishing feature between perception and imagination is a difference of intensity. Alternatively, though confusion becomes inevitable and thus, the difference must be a difference of nature.

The image is not a weakened perception. Also, the image is not a reflection of perception, because it is, in fact, the consciousness, which imagines and perceives it. In each of its two attitudes, the act of consciousness is different and imagining is, therefore, an act of consciousness.

The latest developments of modern psychology and the corresponding contributions of Alain's work and phenomenology have impacted a discussion on the imaginary function of consciousness instead of the image.

Jean-Paul Sartre's perspectives are based on the works of Alain and Edmund Gustav Albrecht Husserl. For Alain, the image does not exist. It is a myth, an illusion. Imagination, for him, is in fact, a mental act, just like perception is a judgment, i.e. a knowledge accompanied by body movements. For example, to imagine an object is to remember that it exists in a certain region and that one must go through a specific path and we can even sketch the movements to turn to the right then to the left. According to Alain, to imagine is always to perceive, which is in alignment with the Empiricist findings. However, the idea "that one sketches movements" should ideally be retained. Likewise, though these are insufficient to account for the imagination, as the discussion does not reduce it to knowledge or a judgment.

In regards to Husserl's phenomenology, "All consciousness is consciousness of something." Consciousness is always intentional, which means, it is aimed at an external object. Perception, as in the imagination consciousness, aims at an object, but essentially always in a different way. To perceive an object implies situating it in the front of our visual field with total availability and attention. While to imagine, is to live in relation to it – as in perception – but while considering it as being absent.

The perspectives of Jean-Paul Sartre state, "imagining is not perceiving," and the concepts pertain two attitudes and two different activities of consciousness. To perceive is the consciousness that aims at the object as present. Perception, conversely, is the function of reality, whereas to imagine it is aimed at the object as not being there; it is to represent it as being absent. For example, my image of Peter is characterized in a certain way of not touching him, not seeing him, and in a way that he has of not being at such a distance. It is so vivid, so touching, and so strong that the image itself reveals its object as not being there.

Therefore, it can be safely inferred that perception and imagination, in context of the same object, are distinguished only by the attitude of consciousness. While, by observation, the object overflows the consciousness with its richness, the object of the image is nothing more than our consciousness of it; and rather, manifests only what we have been able to retain from it.

Imagination supposes a present material object through which the individual aims at the absent object. This material support is termed by Sartre as "the analogon." For example, a lover imagines the other half (who is absent) to be near through a photograph. In case this lover gets carried away in this act of imagining, the lover would sketch in the mind a gesture of embracing or holding the hand, which serves as an analogy.

Similarly, the nocturnal dream is also provoked by a material "analogon." The imagination in the nocturnal dream is triggered and constructed from a noise, a felt movement, a physical discomfort (pain, indigestion), or from a light (which he calls phosphene).

It is annotated, however, that there is no imagination except when the "analogon" is no longer perceived as such; when this matter is erased and the mind retains only that which it symbolizes for the individual. Correspondingly, the significance of individual values and tendencies come into play herein. Explained through the example of the lover's picture that leads the individual's imagination to the loved one. And, where in fact the actual picture, which served as the trigger was forgotten.

These findings account for the distinction between imagination and perception, which are two different attitudes of consciousness in relation to the object. However, it fails to alongside explain the nocturnal imagination, which is also, according to Jean-Paul Sartre, an act of consciousness. In other words, the consciousness in the dream does not consist of a dreamy state, nor it would exist in the hallucination as hallucinated. **The dream is not derived from the activity of consciousness but rather from the intentionality of the subconscious. Freud has explained this masterfully.**

Value and Meaning of the Imagination

The perspective of Jean-Paul Sartre turned the Empiricist point of view upside down. No longer does the imagination reduce to perception but, conversely, if I have to project myself onto the world using imagination, perception then decreases imagination. **I never perceive the world as it is, but as I am.** So, in the Rorschach test, the ink stains serve as an analog to my dreams. Every perception is projective. For example, each individual has his own individual and diverse perspective to see the same drill based on his/her desires, conditioning, fears, and personal wealth.

However, imagination must not be limited to dreams and delusions that further us away from the reality. Besides this form, which Bachelard calls the "nocturnal imagination," we have another form of imagination known as the "construction of the possible." It prepares the knowledge of reality, the one that reconciles itself with reason, which is termed by Bachelard as a creative "diurnal."

The nocturnal form of the imagination can thus be the mistress of falsehoods and errors. However, the creative imagination serves as a source of discovery and creativity. It can be exemplified through the scientist who imagines a hypothesis or a new detour of manipulation, or a new experimentation. It is also, similarly evident in the artist (musician, sculptor, etc.) who creates fiction. However, here the meaning goes deeper than appearances, which is closer to the truth than its reality.

Form and Degree of the Imagination

This section begins with the most inferior (lower) forms, in other words, those that are the least organized.

The first is the wandering imagination (i.e. which does not submit to any discipline and shows no order). Here, memories and images arise, and the subject assists as a simple spectator at the time of their apparition. This imagination deserves to be called the wandering as it develops on the margin of reality. This observed state, especially in the dream and in pathological states of the dreams, people, things, and places, are transformed into each other; they are both this and that. In the pathological case, imaginative creations are the projection of a desire; the desire of a man with no recollection of the real world.

Among the inferior forms, we must mention the imagination of children. Where they transform reality, and the main factor of this transformation is animism. For example, a young girl assuming the boredom of pebbles on the road from always sitting in one place, and so she changed the location of a few. It has been observed that oftentimes, a child's imagination takes the shape of a storytelling. Correspondingly, the child invents a fictional narrative or identifies with made-up characters, with actions that extend for weeks or months. This world created by the child can be explained optimally by the child's tendency and love for the marvelous. The imaginative consciousness of the child naturally resides in the land of wonders. This universe of the marvelous can be truer for the child than the world of common sense.

In adults, however, reverie can still retain many of the characters of the wandering imagination. Despite that, in general, the adult is not absorbed by the imaginary to the same extent as the child. It is noteworthy that the difference between dreams and reverie is that reverie is centered on an object as opposed to the dream. Reverie opens the dreamer to another world, where he/she feels more at ease. Sometimes a daydream absorbs life and rather destroys it. Conversely, though reverie can sometimes play a positive creative role; not in the form of mental vagrancy but in the form of a directed reverie, wherein the subject directs his/her inner visions.

In superior or higher forms, creative imagination forms the obstacle for all inventions. A purely creative imagination would be inexplicable, since, that would necessitate the identification and introduction of the unknown to the known, the strange to the familiar, and the new to the old. Thus, the explanation of a creation precipitates the effect of denying its originality. The creative imagination is not an "ex nihilo" (a Latin phrase that means "out of nothing") creation, as the invention is, indeed, partly explainable. It is related to the personality of the inventor, his/her environment, and to some point in the individual history. The elements of creation are evident in the culture of that period. Therefore, the inventor finds in his/her tendencies, passions, and the needs of the community, the emotional solicitations inspiring his/her creations.

The Elements of the Creative Imagination

Artistic creation evidences an analogous trend. Typically, artists begin their career by imitating their professors, which in fact, follows the refusal of their style. However, subsequently, by opposing their professors, they expose their originality. This transition reveals that human creations do not emerge from ex nihilo, but in fact are the survival products of our creations. The characteristics of the ancient arts partially survive in the modern arts. The fortified castle, for example, presents a loss of its military value because of the development of artillery. Thus, the imagination is creative only by being a continuator.

Scientific discoveries and artistic creations are inspired based on previous cultures. The evolution of science and technology facilitates the discovery of theories, and for this reason, sometimes several scientists working independently of each other, rather, propose the same theory or make the same discovery. For example, Antoine Laurent Lavoisier, a French chemist, and Joseph Priestley, an English chemist, almost simultaneously discovered oxygen!

The Affective Source of the Creative Imagination

Technical inventions are directly linked to needs and tendencies, while all human inventions prolong the biological adaptations of mankind to the environment. The capacity of the invention can be solicited or put to sleep based on the social environment needs. The mechanical inventions weakness' in the Greco-Roman antiquity is explained by the existence of the slaves. Correspondingly, Ribot once said that a French inventor discovered the principle of a repeating rifle model, resulting from hearing a violent speech by Bismarck.

For psychoanalysts, the sources of art creations or expression reside in repressed affectivity. The repressed impulses, which cannot be translated into acts, transform into images by sublimation. The German composer Richard Wagner wrote, "I do not understand how a really happy man could have the idea of making art..."

For instance, the paintings of the French painter Maurice Utrillo are covered with coffee shops, thus depicting the repressed affectivity at a time when his entourage prevented him from drinking coffee. Similarly, the paintings of French painter Henri de Toulouse-Lautrec project the flexible and agile legs of dancers and acrobats, attributing to his very short legs due to a genetic disorder. **The importance of affectivity is apparent not only in the work of art but equally in all imagination forms. It is also that the dream is a compensation for a tendency or an unsatisfied desire for the waking state.**

If affective conditions create the climate of the invention, creative imagination remains an act of thought. It is inseparable from intelligence, i.e. ability to grasp and to assess the relationship between things. The creation of the scientific hypothesis, is, thus an image involving the dissociation of old mental syntheses and the creation of new syntheses. This phenomenon is evident in the genius synthesis of Newton in the hypothesis on universal attraction, and likewise, in Lavoisier discovery of the relation between respiration and combustion.

Marquis de Laplace was an influential French scholar with an imperative contribution to the development of mathematics, statistics, physics, and astronomy. According to him, every invention consisted of the appraisal of ideas capable of joining and which, up to that point, were outlying. Thus, poetry captures all its charm from the rapprochement of different realities. Similarly, for Victor Hugo, a French poet, a rocky mountain surmounted by a cloud appeared like a shepherd wearing a big hat. However, many gave the invention an anti-intellectualist interpretation, **which particularly implies that the processes by which we find are not those by which we prove.** For them, an intuition whose source is attributed to affectivity, to genius, and to chance, underpins the origin of all scientific or artistic inventions. In addition, intuition can be sprung from the subconscious outside of any intellectual approach. However, when emotion creates favorable conditions, intelligence is not absent in the invention. Hence, it is essential, that we do not exaggerate the role of the mysterious subconscious ways.

Abrupt intuition is also known to precede long efforts of the intelligence; exemplified in the case of a person who discovers the next morning the solution of a problem, which he/she sought the previous day. **It is acknowledged that to find without seeking, one must first have sought without finding.** "A fertile intuition is only a starting point of the mind," said Bergson. Intuition, thus, becomes the principle of an authentic invention only through intellectual work. Paul Valéry, a French poet, once said, "If the gods graciously gave us such a first verse, it is up to us to shape the second." Besides the affectivity and the obscure powers of the subconscious, intelligence locates its place in the process of artistic invention and scientific discovery.

Dreams and Reverie (Daydreams)

Dreams and reverie are two phenomena, which essentially, do not have much distinction and are thus often mistaken for each other. This necessitates a separate review and study of each, before finding their unity.

Reverie

In the waking state, the thought is most often tended towards an action, towards a task to be accomplished. However, it sometimes happens that the attention does let loose by distraction or by fatigue, and then the mind is carried elsewhere and lets itself experience the fantasy. This is reverie.

The thought follows the slope of the solicitations of the moment: External action, psychophysiological states, desire, fear, etc. It feeds the imagination and alongside characterizes a magical and particular form of consciousness.

Sometimes a reverie is nothing but relaxation; yes, it can be called the Sunday of thought. This phenomenon can also be fertile and creative, in fact, it is the opposite of a weakness or a failure. Paul Valéry also said,

"Reverie is idle but it is full of power." But reverie can as well indicate psychological weakness; of impotence to think, to concentrate and to pay attention to be present. It is a weakness and, therefore, clearly, it is an illness.

In summary, the reverie is supposed to be superior when it is creative and inferior when it is simple relaxation, and pathological when it manifests as flight and an escape.

The Dream

The dream is the state of sleeping thoughts. According to the dictionary of the French Academy, the relaxation of attention control yields the dream, which is the involuntary assemblage of images and ideas, often incoherent, sometimes clear and continual. It comes to mind during the period of sleep.

The dream presents to us the most passive form of the imagination. Specifically, the images of all kinds of order associate and group themselves around an affective and an organic sensation. The very moment when we dream, we believe we are witnessing real perception, and only after awakening we perceive our illusion. However, sometimes we ask ourselves, during the dream itself, if we are indeed dreaming, which proves the subsistence of our reason and memories from the waking state, during the dream. However, thought intervention, in the midst of dreams, is most often vague and misunderstood. The dream would bring us back to our instincts and our elementary sensitivity, and plunge us back into full concrete realization.

Dream Formation

Towards explaining the dream continuation, physiologists referred to the state of the body and its internal sensation (such as well-being, discomfort, etc.). For example, respiratory and digestive difficulties may lead to nightmares.

It is true that external, sensory stimuli continue to filter through our senses as we dream, but they do not constitute the substantial content of our dreams. Stimuli do not yield the nocturnal dream drama any more than the theater movements producing the play drama, the moment they lift the curtain.

Bergson identified the influence of physiological elements on the dream, but, for him, the dream is above all, a psychological disposition. It indicates a detachment with regard to action, because to dream is to lose interest, and one sleeps when one is disinterested. He further added that this is why some people, are not able to sleep on the eve before an important exam. Bergson explains the formation of the dream but he fails to highlight the content.

According to Freud, the dream is the expression of a desire, suppressed in the waking state and realized in the thoughts of sleep. Yet, in the dreams it is disguised, in order to deceive our senses by a symbolic disguise that makes the dream acceptable.

Despite the high intrigue surrounding this perspective, it is extremely excessive. One fails to perceive the reasons for the dreams to be present an exclusive symbolic manifestation of the repressed tendencies dependent on libido. The dream, in fact, can also be the expression of other dimensions of the person.

The "Medical" Point of View

The medical fraternity presents a diversified perspective about the dream. While few scholars perceive in the peaceful and good sleep a dreamless state, others see in dreams and even nightmares a safety valve and call it paradoxical sleep.

Role and Values of the Dream

1. **The ego escapes into the imagination.**

2. The dream is the revenge of the imagination on intelligence.

3. It is the liberation of the fabulous world of the subconscious

4. We must avoid superstition and credulity (but there are dreams that are premonitory of our deep psyche and our health).

5. **Time is tightened in the dream, and it seems that it is even abolished, which allows consciousness to move in the past and in the future as if it were not a prisoner of the present.**

6. The dream reveals the nocturnal or subconscious aspect of our being as well as a diurnal aspect.

Thus, the role of the dream is to allow the interpretation of the external world based on our personality.

We, therefore, can conclude that imagination has its advantages. It helps the intelligence and it supplies the materials to the thought such as imagining geometric figures in a multi-dimensional space. Imagination is necessary for the human being to escape from the present and therefore, equals freedom. It exercises over us a liberating transformative action. For example, to plan or make projects is to go beyond oneself.

Yet there are also pitfalls for the imagination. The subjective images cause errors and falsehoods; whereas the reality is objective, resistant and present. Under these conditions, the individual may prefer an imaginary world, which is free from the obstacles of the reality. In the extreme cases, the escape into the dream may produce a disappointment or a mental illness, because the reality is totally rejected.

CHAPTER 15:

LANGUAGE, SIGNS, AND SYMBOLS

Mankind walks through a jungle of symbols. In the human world, everything can be answered, evoked, corresponded, and assigned meaning and value to (in relation to consciousness, which is itself a generator of symbols and capable of language and interpretations).

We must distinguish between the natural signs and conventional signs (such as the names of things – for example: A flag, which is a symbol). As a natural sign, one has the signal: It is a phenomenon, which refers to another phenomenon. For example, smoke is a fire signal. As a conventional sign, the symbol invites the consciousness to stop on its sensible aspect to surpass it, analogous to the evocation of the flag. Each countryman, when he/she sees the flag of his/her country, feels pride. Depending on the colors of the flag, other feelings may be invoked. I live in the United Kingdom, and the UK union flag evokes a homeland feeling, and the blue color used in the base is a symbol of vigilance, truth, and loyalty. Another example of symbols and signs is the road signs; each one of them evokes in the individual a different communication. The sign is crossed by the consciousness, which gives it a meaning, an idea. **Thus, it can be safely inferred that the sign is nothing in absence of the meaning to which it refers. However, the thought has no access to meaning without the sign.**

The authentic sign begins at the level of the reflective consciousness, which grasps the true relations between the sign, its signified meaning, and its signifying intention. Correspondingly, language is a system of signs charged with significations for thought, which is reflected in or expressed in it. It pertains to a set of spoken or written signs translating thought through a set of conventional symbols (such as letters) or raised dots (as in the Braille alphabet).

Animal Language and Human Language

The main characteristic of the animal language is that it is expressive but unilateral. Several animals instinctively have a language by which they express their needs and emotions, such as pain, hunger, fear, sexual needs, etc. The first characteristics of this language is that it is innate and instinctive. For example, the cat, calls its kittens by making a sound, the bee has signals by which it indicates the direction and approximate distance of its prey, and monkeys living in groups or in a colony react with screams (as an alarm) on approach of danger.

The language that can be taught to dogs is different from the typical animal language. We train and teach a dog to react in such a determined way to such words and signs; however, the capacity for expression and communication does not increase.

Animal language is limited to a finite number of needs, emotions, and situations. For example, the bee cannot indicate the height of its prey and the animal language is also rarely communicative. Evidently, a rat that has tasted certain bad food is able to bite their companions to prevent them from eating it, however, it is limited from providing an explanation. It is, therefore, a language composed of stereotyped signs and the same sign cannot be attributed to only one meaning inscribed in the genetic language of the animal.

The human language is expressive but also presents the characteristics of being above all, communicative. This communication is bilateral, as it allows for the exchange of information, like ideas and feelings. Thus, the communication of animal language is not a dialogue but unilateral. Language is specifically human only when it exceeds the expressive function when it no longer expresses needs but instead expresses representations. Every representation is mental – it is work, the activity of mind, and consciousness.

Human language is not innate but acquired as the learning is conditioned by the development of mental functions. As a result, the acquisition of language also conditions the individual's intellectual development. Supposedly, thus, if a word has several meanings, and if human language is never limited to another definition of needs and emotions that is because it is symbolic and conceptual.

In fact, the meaning of a word is connected with a sense, i.e. to an idea and not to a thing. For example, the word "table" generally refers to any raised surface that is more or less extended to serve as a support or to a chart as in a table of values, in mathematics. It does not relate to a single known "table" or to a single table form. This word, thus, designates a category of things, instead of a specific thing: **It expresses a concept.**

Language and Society

Language is actually a social fact. It presents the use of speech, constituted by vocal signs and subsequently written ones - as a social institution. This is a collective phenomenon, belonging to the social and coercive group; and thus, it imposes itself on each one of us. It is tied to social reality, as the language of a society consists of all the signs, signifying its needs, its ideas, its morals, its religious and mystical beliefs, its activities, and its knowledge (social, economic, practical, and scientific). Hence, in a word, the language of a society consists of its culture.

In order to grasp this aspect in language, one can compare the languages of a worker, an educated woman, a peasant woman, an official, and a farmer. Each of these characters belongs to a given society and has a social category… **and each of these categories has its own concerns, its own beliefs, and, therefore, its own language.**

Language is also conventional; there is an internal connection between the word and what it symbolizes. This internal link is not found between the word and what it signifies. For example, the daughter of my parents is called "sister" in English, "soeur" in French, and "schwester" in German for the simple reason that there is a convention or a social agreement in them. **That is why language is a conventional sign – the individual receives it and does not create it.**

However, notably, language evolves over time, in accordance with the society's needs and its individual poets, writers, and scholars, responsible for the spread of new words. These words, however, only constitute the language when the whole group (the community) accepts them, recognizes them, and integrates them.

Language is Thought

In the majority of cases, the individuals think of their speech before speaking their mind. Yet, there is no thought without speech. At least, interior to thought is anterior to speech, and it is done in a logical precedence (i.e. of an a priori or deductive condition), thereby, making language possible. The thought is like sap (mineral and vitamins of plants) and signifies the inner nourishing of the word.

The influence of language on thought is said to have a beginning where language allows thought to constitute a body (i.e. thought is incarnated in language). This resultant construct develops, consolidates, and explicates it. Thought before language is nebulous. Language is a means of exchange, marking a vehicle for the transmission of ideas.

Language is also an instrument of analysis. Condillac said, "One cannot speak without decomposing his/her speech into its various elements to express them in turn and speech is the only instrument that allows this analysis of thought." In short, thoughts are organized and disciplined by language.

Functions and Values of Language

It is through language itself that language is learned. Moreover, through language one acquires the culture of the inhabiting group. Correspondingly, it is not enough to communicate and to understand oneself to use the same words – these words must imply the same meanings and the same repercussion in each of the interlocutors. Likewise, it has been observed that the words "mother" and "love" will have different repercussions, based on the individual's oriental or western origins. The difference is also evident, as per the structure of our own environment (society).

Language is the means or a tool, to be understood and understand others, and presents a vessel for the transmission of culture to the new generation. The political, sociological, and scientific philosophical notions are transmitted to us through corresponding symbolic and explanatory words. Technical words in these fields beget precise laws or phenomena that allow researchers to understand each other.

This function of symbolization, possessed by the words explain their evocative character, as they can succeed in the resuscitation of forgotten things in us. Thus, words project a certain magical power because they project the impression of possessing that idea or object. **Hence, when a certain term or word escapes us, it seems that the idea or object behind them escapes us, too.** Mankind has several means to express gestures, mimics, movements, noises, clapping of hands, winks, etc., but the safest, which serves us to express maximal things possible are essentially the words.

Words help us express our joy, love, insult, and hatred (even in the most solitary of solitudes). Similarly, certain verses, especially in poetry, deeply move and impact us by their sounds when they rhyme well. Perhaps, this furnishes a justified explanation of all civilizations' having their own poets. This universal fact regarding the function of symbolizations possessed by the words is, above all, a systematic exploitation. Specifically, it is made by poetry for the purpose of an expression function and as well as the aesthetic function of the language.

The Pitfalls and Perils of Language

We have described language as a mean of formulating and communicating thoughts. But sometimes that mean constitutes a sort of brake or hold, which expresses itself rather than expressing a thought. Thus, a thought cannot be without language, but the language can assume independence in verbalism, which transforms it into empty speech. Thereby, resulting in an insignificant speech quality; as speaking to say nothing is not a sign of intelligence.

Language is also linked to the social reality, which it must express; it is not a docile means to creative innovators or revolutionary geniuses.

While, an idea, a fact, or a new concept fails to find in the language the corresponding or available signs, attributing to its pre-existing link to a predetermined sense. On the other hand, the new signs are incomprehensible to the collective of society and this issue is evident during any attempt at creation or renewal of words.

According to Bergson: 1) The originality of thought makes it incommensurable with language; 2) language cannot express all thought as it is irreducible to language; and 3) all thought is not expressed in language. Thought expresses duration and language expresses space. Therefore, all language for him is a traitor and a liar; as it never faithfully translates thought.

The most serious abuse of all language is **the art of lying, which is made possible through the use of words.** For example, the sophists and the charlatans that utilize language to manipulate words towards morally dubious ends. It must be said that we are all at least sophists when we are led by self-love, passion, or interest.

The Power of Language

Despite the abuse of language, its power cannot be underestimated. Through words, mankind confers a true existence to things by assigning them a name. Naming thus signifies a calling to existence from nothingness. French philosopher George Gusdorf said, "Naming establishes a right to existence. It is words that make things and beings, which define the relationships according to which the order of the world is constituted." Therefore, on addressing something or someone by the name, with which we have identified them or recognized their existence, in some way, we acquire a certain internal power over them. For example, **in poetic and scientific language, mankind in a sense becomes the master of the world and affirms his/her transcendence.**

CHAPTER 16:

<u>CONCEPTUAL INTELLIGENCE</u>

What is the concept of intelligence? In the broad sense, intelligence is the set of mental functions, with the exclusive objective of knowledge. In the narrow sense, it refers to the faculty of understanding (i.e. to acquire links, relations, rapports, etc.).

Intelligence is the capacity that makes thought possible and intervenes only when no instinct or habit corresponds to the situation of an individual. It has a practical function of adaptation, and it is in this sense that one can speak of animal intelligence. The animal may be in a new situation, with an obligation to conform to the new surroundings.

The discussion raises the questions: What are the characteristics of human intelligence? What is the material object of thought? Are there many forms of intelligence? It is through asking these questions that we can find our answers.

Intelligence can be studied from two viewpoints – its mechanism and aptitudes. This is illustrated in the following statements: 1) "Man is intelligent" and 2) "Such a man is intelligent."

1) "Man is intelligent" designates human intelligence in general; its mechanism, as opposed to the "animal instinct."

2) "Such a man is intelligent" designates an individual subject to his/her aptitude.

The Mechanism of Intelligence

Sensorimotor intelligence appears in the higher animals and manifests itself through an intuitive adaptation to a new situation, however, unlike the instinctual response; it is taken prisoner by its stereotype schema.

Sensory-motor intelligence invents a new pattern of behavior with its intelligence limited in the genetic structure (i.e. the form of perceptions of movements). It is always special, without overall representation, and always practical.

Wolfgang Köhler was a German psychologist who experimented with chimpanzees. He placed food on the higher ground and found that when he placed wooden crates and sticks in their cage, then the chimpanzees stacked these crates to climb to reach them. Similarly, when the food was placed on the ground outside of the cage, they used the wood sticks to lengthen the reach of their arms. He posited that animal intelligence could be, thus, determined as an ability to establish relationships between things deposited in a determinate space. The intuitions of the chimpanzees indicate the intuitions of behaviors; that act directly without these actions being preceded by mental representations, interrogations, or abstract ideas. Therefore, the chimpanzees here did not first construct a plan, which was subsequently executed.

In a seperate experiment, now adding the bait before the food that were placed in front of the cage. Chimpanzees here needed to execute abstract mental work, and thus required the use of a few notions, especially a temporal one. For example, the chimpanzee would first need to grab a stick to reposition the bait, and then turn to grabs a second stick to get the banana . However, all these elements may remain inaccessible and impossible to execute for the animal. Köhler concluded that animals' intelligence shows a capacity for space restructuring and observing things combined with their relations. **Thus, it can be inferred that the structuring of time that requires mental representation and the use of concepts belong to mankind alone.**

The Conceptual Human Intelligence

Conceptual intelligence is unique to mankind and this can be attributed to the acquisition of language. It perceives intellectual relations, proceeds through analysis and synthesis, and finally grasps structured and coherent systematic wholeness. It has no limits because it creates means, and is concurrently practical as well as theoretical.

However, practical intelligence precedes theoretical intelligence in time. The intelligence of the child is at first practical, wherein the child can link behaviors but not abstract ideas. The same stands true of the history of humanity, and we find this intelligence is practiced amongst the primitive man, which precedes the theoretical intelligence and evidence preparation. Theoretical intelligence relates abstract notions, manipulates concepts, and is conceptual in nature. Additionally, human intelligence, which has become theoretical, dominates time and can represent the present, the past, and the future.

Intellectual Aptitudes: The Study of the Degrees and Forms of Intelligence

The degrees of intelligence involve the determination of the skill levels through the use of the psychological method of testing. This method consists of preparing a set of questions (considered as characteristic for a given age bracket amongst mankind and where three-quarters of that age group are capable of responding to it) and having people answer them.

French psychologists, Alfred Binet and Theodore Simon created the Binet-Simon method of determining a person's IQ or intelligence quotient. This formula elicits a quantitative measure of one's intellectual ability through the relationship between his/her mental age and his/her actual age, which is formulated by the following equation:

$$IQ = \text{mental age} \div \text{physical age} \times 100.$$

If $IQ = 100$, intelligence is normal, if $IQ < 100$, intelligence is viewed as abnormal, and if $IQ > 100$, intelligence is viewed as gifted (or genius).

This Binet-Simon method of intellectual tests has been found to be better suited for children as compared to adults, because, for adults, it detects the lower forms of intelligence. Modern intelligence tests no longer compute IQ scores this way. New tests have since evolved, and particularly, some tests for adults help them orient themselves to make an informed choice for their vocation and career, i.e. identify their ideal jobs and subsequently pursue the same.

Forms of Intelligence:
Special and Qualitative Forms

There are three specialized forms of intelligence: practical, theoretical, and imaginative.

Practical intelligence is the ability to solve concrete problems and adapt to new situations. It reasons on objects and tools. It is a utilitarian intelligence – devoted – and is manifested in the politician, businessman, technician, etc.

Theoretical intelligence is the aptitude to pose and to solve abstract problems. It reasons on ideas, and it is indifferent. It is manifested in the philosopher, in the scientist, and in the mathematician.

Imaginative (or artistic) intelligence is the ability to reason and think with images. It is demonstrated in artists in all fields, such as poets, musicians, painters, sculptors, filmmakers, etc.

It is possible that these three forms of intelligence can coexist in the same individual; however, the predominance of one allows the orientation or the choice of a profession or a career.

Qualitative Forms or Attitudes

The spirit of finesse is characterized by the righteousness and delicacy of the spirit, the analytical spirit.

The spirit of geometry is a spirit that seeks distinct and clear abstract principles. It is characterized by amplitude (broad mind) and the vigor of mind, which we can call a synthetic spirit.

The two above attitudes may as well be evident in the same person; however, they would create lacunae or a defect. The synthetic spirit operates via sets of brain rules-governed operations, while conversely, the spirit of finesse seeks spirituality and self-mastery. Therefore, the two inhabiting the same person can cause considerable cognitive dissonance.

Other Types of Intelligence

Assimilative intelligence is the ability to understand the theoretical reasoning of a system already discovered and supposed.

Creative intelligence is the aptitude for discovery and intellectual creation. Notably, the creative intelligence is the highest and purest form, involving all other forms of intelligence.

In order to understand intelligence and grasp it in its depth and its different dimensions, we need to compare the two following verbs: **To understand and to explain.**

To understand is to grasp things from our inner being, in their rapport, and in their relationship between them to the world and of their first truth (i.e. their primary cause). To understand is to justify something. That is to say, the mind is satisfied only when it has found the ultimate reason for things, which indicates their explanation and their underlying reason. To understand is to discover a sense, to grasp instinctively, and to penetrate things from within. In short, to be intelligent is to be reasonable.

To explain is to interpret things from the outside without being able to grasp their logical and dialectical links. This sort of intelligence is superficial.

CHAPTER 17:

NEURONS AND THE BRAIN

What are Neurons?

Neurons are nerve cells that can transmit electrical and chemical signals. Their function is to transmit information in both chemical and electrical forms throughout the entire body and constitute the basic building block of the nervous system.

Each of our neurons has a specific voltage, which is able to change with the flow of ions, in or out of the cell. The moment a neuron's voltage has reached a certain desired level, it sends an electrical signal to other cells in the network, which causes them to repeat the process. Correspondingly, brainwaves can be measured with the electrical signals fired concurrently by many of our neurons. These brainwaves, as they oscillate at different frequencies, get classified in bands such as alpha, theta, and gamma. Each one of them is associated with a different task and they underpin nearly all the operations of the minds, including attention, intelligence, and memory. Brainwaves ignore irrelevant signals and allow our brain cells to tune into the frequency corresponding to their particular tasks, similar to how a radio dial tunes in on different waves to pick up a specific radio station.

Will is merely the drive to reduce the dissonance between each of our active neural circuits. The transfer of information between neurons is optimized with a synchronized activity of the neurons. This is the same reason why we experience cognitive dissonance, which demonstrates as the frustration caused by two simultaneous contradictory ideas.

What Carries Our Nervous System?

Your spinal cord carries the nerves that control all your movements. Your brain is the most complicated part of your nervous system. It receives information via the spinal cord, directly from your ears, eyes, nose, and mouth – as well as from the rest of your body. This information subsequently helps you react, remember, think, and plan, and then send out the appropriate instructions to your body.

It is through the nervous system that we communicate with the outside world. It receives information through our senses, from the skin, joints, and muscles of our body. This information is then processed in the central nervous system (CNS), which goes from the spinal cord to the brain. Thereafter it triggers reactions in us, such as a muscle movement. For example, if I put my hand over a candlelight, my arm will instinctively pull back with the heat sensation and the nerves simultaneously will send signals of pain to my brain.

The nervous system is a combination of the central nervous system (CNS) and the peripheral nervous system (PNS). The central nervous system includes the nerves in the brain and spinal cord. All of the other nerves in the body are part of the PNS.

Science presents to us two distinctions: It says one is the voluntary nervous system and the other is the involuntary nervous system. The former is a somatic nervous system, which controls all that we can influence and are conscious of, and the latter is the autonomic nervous system, which, in fact, regulates the processes in our body, regardless our awareness and what we are unable to influence consciously. Like, the biological parts of us that regulates our breathing, heartbeat, and metabolic processes and this is entirely achieved via signals sent from the brain. In addition, reversed communication is also evident, for example, such as when your bladder requests to visit the restroom. The involuntary nervous system reacts promptly to bodily changes; for example, the body increases the blood circulation to your skin, when it is too hot, thereby causing you to sweat and cool down your body.

Both the CNS and PNS have voluntary as well as the involuntary parts. However, whereas these two parts are closely associated in the CNS they are usually separate in other areas of the body.

The 3 Parts of the Nervous System

The involuntary nervous system is made up of three parts: (i) the sympathetic nervous system; (ii) the parasympathetic nervous system; (iii) and the enteric (gastrointestinal) nervous system.

The sympathetic nervous system prepares the body for physical and mental activity. It makes the heart beat faster and stronger, opens the airways so the body can breathe more easily, and inhibits digestion.

The parasympathetic nervous system is responsible for bodily functions when we are at rest. It stimulates digestion, activates various metabolic processes, and helps us relax. The sympathetic and parasympathetic nervous systems usually are observed to conduct opposite operations in the body, however, they sometimes complement each other, too.

The enteric (gastrointestinal) nervous system (ENS) is a separate nervous system that contains as many neurons as the spinal cord and is often called our second brain. It controls the reflexes of the gastrointestinal system to a great extent, as it autonomously regulates bowel motility in the digestion. Recent research shows that the ENS seems to also play an important role in our physical and mental well-being. It can work both independently of and in conjunction with the brain in the head and, although you are not conscious of your gut "thinking," the ENS helps you sense environmental threats and then influences your response. "A lot of the information that the gut sends to the brain affects well-being, and doesn't even come to consciousness," says Michael Gershon at Columbia-Presbyterian Medical Center, New York.

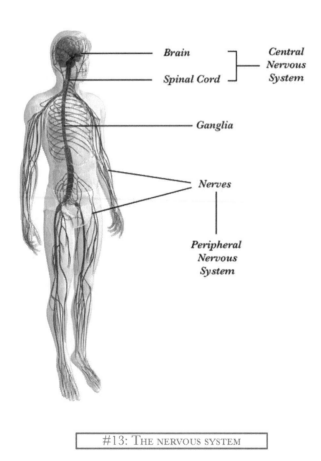

#13: The nervous system

The Brain

The human brain is a network of approximately one hundred billion neurons. Different experiences create different neural connections in our brain that initiate different thoughts, emotions, and behaviors – all which constitute our character and personality. Those neural connections can become strengthened or weakened, depending on which are more stimulated and this is termed as neuroplasticity. For example, someone who trains to be a painter will create stronger neural connections between the two hemispheres of their brain. It has been evidenced that virtually any sort of talent or skills can be created through training. Rudiger Gamm, a hopeless student, who used to fail at basic math, later went on to train his abilities and became a famous human calculator capable of performing significantly complex mathematics. Correspondingly, emotional experience, behaviors, attitudes, rationality, outlooks and many more work exactly in the same way. These are neural connections that can be trained and strengthened. **Therefore, at any given time, whatever you are doing, in the process, you are physically modifying your brain to become better at it. Moreover, since this is such a foundational mechanism of the brain, being self-aware can, in turn, greatly enrich our life experience.**

"The great pleasure and feeling in my right brain is more than my left brain can find the words to tell you," said Roger Sperry, a neuropsychologist, and neurobiologist, who won the 1981 Nobel Prize in Physiology and Medicine for his work with split-brain research.

Our brain has two hemispheres (the right and the left) that work together independently and can compensate for the other in the instance of a brain liaison in one half. However, each is specialized in different tasks. The right side of the brain takes care of the space perception tasks, artistic tasks, musical tasks, and more, while the left side of the brain is normally specialized in taking care of the analytical and verbal tasks.

Similarly, according to Joseph E. LeDoux, an American neuroscientist, if the left cerebral hemisphere were to be disconnected from the right one, as evident in the case of split-brain patients, the left-brain will not miss the right part, irrespective of the profound changes in their perception. The patient would still be able to talk and think from the left while their right hemisphere would have very limited cognitive capacities. One of the consequences is that they can no longer describe the right half of someone's face; however practically as they will never see it as a problem, therefore they will never mention it, or even realize that something has changed. Vilayanur Subramanian Ramachandran, an Indian-born neuroscientist, confirms this and adds that because this affects more than just their perception of the real world; it also applies to their mental images. **It is not just a sensory problem but, in fact, also enables a fundamental change in their consciousness.**

Despite what we know about the two sides of our brain, the following logical, unanswered question remains: Why are some functions only represented on one side of the brain?

The Nature of the Brain and Consciousness

Our brain's left cerebral hemisphere is majorly responsible for creating a coherent belief system and controls the right side of the body. It is dominant in language functions, such as processing what you hear and regulating the majority of speech functions. It primarily though pertains to all functions related to logic and is responsible for folding all of our experiences into the pre-existing belief system. However, when they don't fit, they are simply denied. This is counterbalanced by the right cerebral hemisphere, which has the opposite tendency and thus coordinates the left side of the body. Specifically, it performs tasks pertaining to creativity and art.

The left hemisphere's primary function is to preserve the existing beliefs and conversely, the right hemisphere relentlessly tries to challenge the status quo. It is propelled by the idea to assist our progress out of old dysfunctional beliefs in the context of contemporary times and needs. Correspondingly, when the conflicting variations in any two-antithetical beliefs become too large, the right hemisphere forces a revision in our worldview. This process usually is resulted from the experience of psychological pain, emotional trauma, or some other type of suffering. **However, when our beliefs are tenaciously rooted in the ego or subconscious, then the right hemisphere may not succeed in overruling our denial.** This fact creates in individuals a profound confusion when mirroring others, as the brain enters in a cognitive dissonance state when challenged with differing perspectives.

In consequence, while in such a state, our entire consciousness that constitutes all the active circuits in our brain would be limited only to activity regarding our mirror neurons. Thus, it would limit our consciousness to these very specific brain synergies and functions. For example, just as when we experience thirst, our consciousness consists mostly of neural interactions for drinking water. In fact, when thirst occurs, all the various zones of the brain become active or inactive and collaborate without a core. Thirst is not sourced from some core self-giving commands to different cerebral areas. Precisely as the billions of pixels on a screen, when they are expressed in unity, they become a recognizable image or the example of dotted paintings where their unity constitute an image, as in the work of the French post-impressionist painter Georges-Pierre Seurat; one of his famous dotted painting is called "A Sunday Afternoon on the Island of la Grande Jatte." The total confluence of neural interactions expresses itself as consciousness. At any moment, we are in fact a different expression, a different image when mirroring, when thirsty, when hungry, and when reading this book. Every second, we are in a different frame of mind as we go through different states of consciousness.

With the use of our mirror neurons to observe ourselves, we are able to construct the concept of an identity. However, it is imperative to perceive ourselves via a scientific perspective, which projects a completely diverse view. We are then exposed to a network of synthesis, correlations, and synergies between neurons, and the brain operates somehow similar to what a computer program, although, way more sophisticated. The neural synergies that produce our oscillating consciousness go far beyond just our own neurons. We are equally the result of the cerebral hemispheres interacting electrochemically, as these senses connecting our neurons to other neurons in our environment via the mirroring neurons, in conjunction with other physical or metaphysical senses. Nothing is external and this is not a hypothetical philosophy; it is the basic property of mirror neurons, which allow us to understand ourselves through the analogy with others. Perceiving this neural activity, as independent and your own, while excluding the environment, would thus constitute a major fallacy.

According to several neuroscientists, the human brain is, in fact, a "biological computer" and the "consciousness of humans" is a program run by the quantum computer located inside the brain that continues to exist even after we "die." As Sir Roger Penrose, a mathematical physicist at Oxford University and Dr. Stuart Hameroff, an American Physicist and Emeritus in the Department of Anesthesiology and Psychology, have ventured in a Quantum Theory of Consciousness in which they state that the soul is maintained in micro-tubules of the brain cells. They have implied, "that after people die, their soul comes back to the universe; it does not die."

Mirror or Empathetic Neurons and Consciousness

Mirror neurons were discovered in 1980 by the Italian scientist Giacomo Rizzolatti. They evidently constitute one of the most important discoveries in the last decade of neuroscience, as recent neurological research has confirmed the existence of empathetic mirror neurons. Mirror neurons are cells that fire during both the execution and observation of a specific action. When we experience an emotion or perform an action, specific neurons fire. But when we observe someone else performing this action, or when we imagine it, many of the same neurons fire again as if we were performing the action ourselves.

Several researchers argue that mirror neurons are critical for various aspects of our social cognition life. The ability to follow the sequence of actions of another individual and predict these sequences develops in us the ability to determine their implications. Therefore, when we perceive the intention behind an action, we enable the mirror neurons and a different system in the brain is activated. That ability to understand the sensory implications of the motor actions we perceive allows us to create a map in the mind, which correlates the neuron firing patterns with the mirroring neurons in the brain, that creates a representation of their intention in our heads. These empathy neurons play an imperative role in the imitation and understanding of the actions of others, connecting us to them, and allowing us to feel what others feel. And since these neurons respond to our imagination, we can experience emotional feedback from them as if it came from someone else.

According to V. S. Ramachandran, this system facilitates the process of self-reflection in humans. The mirror neurons are unable to differentiate between it and others and this underpins our dependency on social validation and our strong need for conformance and acceptance. We are in a perpetual duality between how we see ourselves and how others see us, which can often result in confusion, in terms of identity and self-esteem. And brain scans validate that we experience these negative emotions even prior to our awareness of them. The good news is that, when we are self-aware, we can alter the misplaced emotions because we are then in control of the causal and underpinning thoughts. This is a neurochemical consequence on how memories of emotions become labile when revived and how these memories are reinstated via protein synthesis.

Self-observing (introspection and retrospection), self-reflecting, and self-awareness have a profound impact on affecting the changes in the way our brain works. It activates the self-regulating neo-critical regions, which gives us an incredible amount of control over our feelings as well as the understanding of others and ourselves. Every time we go through self-observation, we enforce our neuron's connections. Therefore, our rationality and emotional resilience are strengthened, similar to when an athlete trains hard to become an Olympic champion. When we are not being self-aware, most of our thoughts and actions are impulsive, and then driven by our subconscious pilot (detailed in Chapter 4). The idea that we are randomly reacting and not making conscious choices – which we discussed in the introduction of the book, where scientists determined that as much as 95% of our actions are made out of automated and subconscious expressions – represents an instinctively frustrating proof to mankind. **The ego resolves this frustration by creating explanations for our behavior and physically rewriting it in our memories through memory reconsolidation and deceiving us into believing that we were in control of our actions.** This is also called "backwards rationalization" and it can leave most of our negative emotions unresolved, suppressed in the subconscious and ready to be triggered at any particular time. These subsequently, constitute our constraints and the fuel of troubles or confusions to our psyche. Our brain continues to justify our irrational behavior until we resolve the root of these confusions. This nearly schizophrenic and complex subconscious behavior is the outcome of a vastly parallel-distributed system in our brain.

The manifestation of a unity in the human being is, in fact, each of these separate circuits being enabled and being expressed at one particular moment in time. Every single experience simultaneously physically changes our neural connections and expands our main operating system, i.e. our consciousness. Direct modifications of any of those processes can impact surreal consequences that bring into question of where consciousness resides within the individual. Thus, we can confidently infer a lack of center of consciousness, and an individual is a unity as much as mankind, through our collective subconscious or consciousness, and so is this entire universe. We just experience difficulties perceiving these correlations, connections, influences, relations, effects, etc. due to our ego as well as the operations of our linear perspectives.

Defensiveness and the Self

We are born with an innate defensive state of mind to ensure our survival, but where does it come from? And how does it stop us from realizing our potential?

Defensiveness is the body's natural response to external stimuli, which are in contradiction with the current belief system of an individual. When we are confronted with differences in opinion, and when we feel that our thoughts must be protected from the influence of others, we react defensively. Our body reacts chemically, as though we have been literally threatened. And relatively, even though this threat originated from totally harmless opinions or thoughts that we might otherwise rationally agree with and find insightful or helpful. In these specific conditions, neurons and neurotransmitters (such as norepinephrine) trigger our defensive state. The same chemicals that are released in the brain try to ensure our survival in dangerous situations. This also causes the more primitive part of the brain to interfere with rational thinking, and the limbic system then is able to knock out most of our working memory, physically causing narrow-mindedness. We can observe the exact same state when someone is stubborn in a discussion. No matter how valuable an idea is, the brain has trouble processing it when it is in such a state.

Using defensiveness blocks our feelings, but it doesn't make them disappear. Being able to recognize this defensiveness state can actually unblock those feelings. The only way to overcome them is to deal specifically, with each one by addressing it at its root. The moment you extract a seed rooted in the subconscious, that you were not aware of and bring it to consciousness, it ceases to be a blind spot. Defense mechanisms emerge from childhood as we learn to cope with the external world. However, when things get tough, they take on a life of their own, becoming a suit of armor to "protect" us.

Social validation increases the level of dopamine and serotonin in the brain. Therefore, when we express ourselves and our views are appreciated, the brain evidences a decrease in the defense chemicals. Then dopamine neurotransmission activates the reward neurons, which makes us feel empowered and increases our self-esteem. **This allows us to let go of emotional fixations and become self-aware more easily.**

Self-esteem or self-belief is closely linked to the neurotransmitter serotonin levels in our system. When the lack of it takes on severe proportions, it often leads to depression, self-destructive behavior, and even suicide. Our beliefs have a deep and profound impact on the chemistry of our body and this has not yet been well understood by science. This is why the placebos can be very effective, as the placebo effect works based on a person's expectations. For example, if an individual is certain of the effects of a pill, then it is possible that the body's own chemistry would cause them the same exact effect.

It has been observed that mankind is in a perennial attempt to get comfortable in each moment and every situation in life. By design, life offers us challenges that we need to overcome. Correspondingly, the positivity of the experience from exercising can only be appreciated if those feelings are compared with the inactive state. You can only appreciate wisdom when you are experiencing life. It is imperative to add that, when we are not self-aware, our perception of reality is not the entire truth but only our subconscious projection of the self into that portion of reality.

Who, Me?

I can almost hear you saying, *Who me? I am not defensive!* Yet we all are, in one way or another. Therefore, the next time you are tempted to engage in a defensive act, observe and notice how the execution of the act, subsequently makes you feel. Keep a close attention on the response and the response mechanisms of your body: How your breathing quickens, your heart races, and/or you may suddenly feel hot or cold.

Admitting that we are defensive is the first step to overcoming this limiting reaction. Let me tell you that anger is the worst thing for a human; it destroys your connection to yourself and others. Rationally, you agree with me. However, moments or days later, you may encounter a situation that manages to evoke your anger. This happens, despite your understanding of the negative and detrimental effects of anger. The same analogy applies to the expression of being defensive. Defensiveness occurs due to the subconscious seed that is triggered by an external stimulus for you to become conscious of, and it challenges you to transform it.

In such a scenario, the best favor you can do for yourself is to tune into your feelings or emotions. Slowing down or pausing and taking a breath before you react, especially when you are angered, can achieve this. When you are moved in such a way, your hackles go up. Start to understand your defensive mechanisms by recognizing them from the list below. **If you are unable to identify with any of them, then, clearly denial is your number one defense mechanism.**

- Withdrawing into silence
- Endless explaining
- Holding a grudge
- Obsessive thinking
- Playing the victim
- Inappropriate laughing
- Taking offense
- Cynicism
- Sarcasm
- Harshness
- Blaming
- Shaming
- Preaching
- Trivializing
- Loss of humor

CHAPTER 18:

<u>CHARACTER AND PERSONALITY</u>

We have hitherto looked at the scattered and distinct psychological phenomena. However, the profound unity of mankind invites us to consider it now as the integral subject of these phenomena, in fact, as the source of which these phenomena are its expressions. Thus, we must seek the specific nature of this subject (a person). The analysis leads us to consider it in the context of individual psychology, thereby, emphasizing the importance attached to the notions of character and personality.

We are here in an abstract function but are faced by subjects, yet these subjects are not considered to be individuals instead pertain to specific types of character and personality. Thus, in order to know these types, one mut begin by revealing his/her natural structure, derived from his/her heredities and what we call character. This individuality must then be analyzed, insofar as it constitutes the totality of the self, namely, the study of personality constructed in the past through education and society.

Character

In the broad sense, the word character can be reduced to the individual psychological complex and it does not designate the whole personality, but what distinguishes it or individualizes it. In the narrow sense, character signifies a set of congenital dispositions, which always inclines us towards the same direction. Ribot considers the character to be "reduced to that, which is innate." The mark of a true character appears from childhood and lasts throughout one's life. Correspondingly, the character is everything that is innate in an individual, thereby, constituting its first nature.

Thus, the idea of character implies a reference to the individualist and his/her specific peculiarity or difference from all the others. These individual properties are numerous. In the same regard, in order to constitute a systematic knowledge of human conduct, it is essential to consider some general and constant properties, which intervene in the majority of cases. What are these general factors?

The Factors or Properties
Constituting the Character

Extensive literature review reveals three properties: (i) activity, (ii) emotiveness, and (iii) resonance.

Activity: This refers to a natural disposition to act. By virtue of this definition, one possesses a criterion, which impacts the possibility of recognition and is related to the external obstacle. For the so-called active individual, the obstacle pushes him/her to act; it reinforces in the individual the dynamism of the action. The inactive, on the other hand, is discouraged before the obstacle. The active individual is generally occupied, decided, independent, an achiever, is a good observer, and has a present mind.

Emotivity: An individual is said to be emotional when an event produces in him/her a more or less strong agitation. The emotional individual is easily troubled by this disorder, which translates into visual signs (such as mobility anxiety, violence, a tendency for exaggeration, and for categorical affirmation). While the non-emotional is a cold individual, he/she is not easily troubled by the events of the external world.

Resonance: This is the individualistic way of reacting to an event and the responsiveness can either be primary or secondary. The primary are fast to react, they live in the present and are renewed with it, although, it is done in a superficial way and they are inconstant in the effect of any project. The secondary is the individual with delayed reactions and for whom the past never ceases to resonate. They have lasting impressions; he/she is usually laid-back, calm, conservative, and strongly attached to the past. Such a person is often a prisoner trapped by prejudices and routines.

Character Types

According to these three constituent properties, and based to their possible combinations, the French psychologist René Le Senne has distinguished eight character types: Passionate, Choleric, Phlegmatic, Sanguine, Sentimental, Nervous, Apathetic, and Amorphous.

The Passionate (EAS = emotional-active-secondary function): This type of individual is characterized by an extreme tension of the whole person and shows an active concentration on a precise goal. This individual has the qualities of being domineering, organized, sometimes selfish, helpful, good with respect to others, and gifted in extraordinary labor. The passionate has a vast intelligence and a remarkable interest in the philosophical, religious, and social problems. In addition, the passionate showcases a deep sense of greatness.

The Choleric (EAP = emotional, active, primary function): This type of individual has an apparent vitality, is impulsive and shows him or herself as generous, cheerful in society, and happy to live. He/she is generally enthusiastic, extroverted, talkative, and sociable, with a slight tendency for exaggeration. A Choleric often lacks discipline and patience and has a keen interest in the politics and social affairs. A Choleric loves people has a strong sexuality, believes in progress, and is often endowed with oratorical aptitude (an interest in philosophy or literature), albeit superficial. Also, a Choleric is often gifted with a very good musical ear.

The Phlegmatic (nEAS = non-emotional, active, secondary function): This type of individual is usually calm, cold, and objective. He/she speaks quietly and slowly, using gentle gestures. He/she is an honorable individual of habit, respects principles and customs, is punctual and methodical, constantly occupied, patriotic, reflective, conservative, and severe with regard to children. He/she is patient, tenacious, and generally well-endowed for the abstract, mathematical, and physical sciences.

The Sanguine (nEAP = non-emotional, active, primary function): This type of individual has a robust activity, is often superficial, anxious or worried, and is inconsistent in his conduct. He/she has a well-developed analytical intelligence, knows how to handle people, is a skilled diplomat, and is an excellent trader. He/she has respect for the great principles, yet the principle fundamental to him/her is: "We must save the appearances."

The Sentimental (EnAS = emotional, non-active, secondary function): This type of individual is very sensitive to external events, has a likeness for loneliness and meditation, is usually shy, and withdraws into him/herself. The Sentimental is very mundane, clumsy, stubborn, prudent, and not very authoritarian. His/her ambition remains at the stage of inspiration. Individualistic, he/she manifests a taste for nature and has a keen interest in the ethical problems. The Sentimental may be displeased with him/herself and is very inclined to boredom.

The Nervous (EnAP = emotional, non-active, primary function): This type of individual would have a deep look, manifests strong organic needs, has an early curiosity, and a highly changing mood. He/she draws attention and is indifferent to objectivity; the nervous need to embellish reality. Gifted for art, seductive, not persevering and mistrustful, the Nervous also love the game of chance, work irregularly, have reactive impulsiveness and poetic feelings, and talk much about themselves. Very inconsistent in their affection, they quickly abandon things or people.

The Apathetic (nEnAS = non-emotional, non-active, secondary function): This type of individual has a closed personality, speaks very little and without enthusiasm, is usually dark, often turns to him/herself, and is a slave of his/her habits. The Apathetic is usually conservative and prefers routine.

The Amorphous (nEnAP = non-emotional, non-active, primary function): This type of individual is served by organic interests, is usually lazy and likes being at ease. Negligent and indifferent in society, he/she sometimes shows passive obstinacy. The Amorphous is of average intelligence, is not very curious, possesses long and superficial judgments, and is after selfish pleasures.

The Personality

Personality is the richest and most significant notion in psychology. It is the most complex organization, which essentially, consists of the unity of the entire psyche, it is the unique "Me" which is expressed outwards of what we can identify too as our individual ego; thus, it is the combination of all combinations.

The problem of personality is not specifically restricted to the psychological domain, and in fact, also appears to be a problem within the confines of psychology and metaphysics. Thus, on a purely psychological ground, one may propose to study the essential characteristics of the "ego," its formation, its evolution, and the probable influencing disturbances or issues.

Therefore, the personality of an individual with characteristics of identity, unity, and autonomy is not realized spontaneously. Similarly, if the personality in all its comprehension exists in reflective consciousness, and in the active and living synthesis of several different elements, the personality must necessarily vary according to the degree of reflections and the power of synthesis. Personality is, therefore, the result of a construction – it is a conquest and a creation. Naturally, every construction is an effort and requires materials, without which, construction would be unachievable. For an in-depth discussion, we must go through the essential elements of the construct of our personality.

What Factors are Involved In This Construction?

We can distinguish between two groups of factors: extrinsic factors (organism and environment) and intrinsic factors (basic provision and voluntary effort).

Personality and Organism

Organic individuality is an important factor, with a significant influential role in the formation of our personality. The nervous system, in particular, centralizes and coordinates activities and constitutes the fundamental organic element. Therefore, the good or bad physiological functioning of the body plays an important role in the construct of the personality. Our core organism is the support of our personality; and is the support of our mental, moral, and intellectual life. The intersecting relationship between the organism and the personality is reflexive and one cannot exist in a balanced state in absence of the other.

Through my body, I experience the action of the world on me and vice-versa my action on the world. Through the body and its language, I know others, and others know me. Likewise, by drawing comparisons between the image of my body with that of others, I become aware of my individuality and my distinct appearance. The influences of sex, gender, traits, sensory functions, age, and others, assign our personality an individual appearance that classifies us in a distinct human category. Even our clothes touch us closely because they become a kind of a second skin for our bodies, thus signifying our identity, in the eyes of others. They translate our tastes and, to a certain extent, materialize our character.

The unity and identity of the personality are largely a reflection of the unity and identity of the body. And, that is why the physiological disorders, illness, and fatigue profoundly modify our personality. Furthermore, the disturbances of perception lead to disorders of feelings.

It goes without saying that the changes of the body are not all devaluing because some have happy effects on personality. Likewise, if illness exacerbates character and timidity is explained by muscular weakness; good health, on the contrary, makes us optimistic and accords us the joy of living. In an analogous way, we can rejoice in certain changes such as a cure or a happy modification of our hairstyle, after a spa day, and others.

Personality and Society

Even more than the organism, the environment imposes on the person a definite form. Therefore, the environment must be understood in the broadest sense, in order to, understand the family, the social, and even the national environments. The personality is shaped and enriched by the imperative influence of social factors. Correspondingly, we can go as far as to say that mankind is not the same in two different societies. The action of the environment is manifested via the indigenous manners, traditions, language, various constraints, and also by collective imperatives. We know that some sociologists have exaggerated the role of society in the formation of personality. For example, according to the French sociologist, David Émile Durkheim, our consciousness of our psyche "ego" or personality is a social product.

For Abram Kardiner, an American anthropologist and psychoanalyst, our social situation – in particular, our economic condition greatly impacts our personality. These factors are the social institutions that model the basic personality.

Particular attention must be paid to the influence of the family environment, parent's education, and the professional environment on the individual personality. On review, the influence of the family environment sustains as the most important and the most durable. And as evidenced by the fact that the children will receive habits, customs, beliefs, and values from their family. Similarly, family conflicts profoundly determine the personality construct.

In a still more precise way and against the opinion of certain thinkers who conceive the personality as a kind of closed domain that blossoms by only internal meditation, the most naive observation proves that the authentic personality cannot live and develop singularly by society and communication with others. However, if we designate by the social

"Me" all that exists in the human personality comes only from society, therefore, this would imply that the social "Me" is the totality of the self (the wholeness of a person). The personality of an individual is largely conditioned and shaped by the life of his/her parents, his/her birth – circumstances and surroundings, the ways or types of feeding, and education. The form of the family customs, laws, habits, and more, which are models of the influence of society on our active, emotional, and intellectual lives; show that there is no possible existence for mankind without a human society.

The intersecting relationship between society and personality is not simple and presents a unique meaning. It designates, on one hand, the elements of social origin in my personality and, on the other hand, the elements of my personality, which allow me a social role and contact with others.

Every individual is born on a date, in a certain city, and from or into families with either both parents or one. My name, my family, my social background, and where I was raised, invariably determine the core of my personality. Concurrently, we mingle with other collectives, and accordingly, we have to deal with other individuals and maintain our existence within a society, where we are led to live very diverse relations. Our personality is largely shaped by our character (i.e., by the role that we fulfill in society). The character brings to the personality the elasticity required to assert itself to others and to itself. Mankind is, above all, the individual of his/her own occupation and deprived of its social function, is somehow depersonalized.

Personality is the Individual History

For one part, our individual story shapes us and this holds true, not only for the manifested elements of the personality but also all the suppressed experiences. However, these events that took place in our past do not create our personality. Nonetheless, they are a part of our innate character that deeply influences our personality. The study of twins brings us excellent results in that matter; it allows us to study innate dispositions and acquired attitudes. Their inheritances and their organic constitution are identical but their distinguishing elements of personality are sourced from society, individual experiences, and the environment in general.

The same events take on a different meaning for individuals of different character. Everyone lives the world in his/her own way. Naturally, to construct a personality for him/herself, an individual must realize and achieve a self. This realization depends on the general character as well as on the will, insofar as it assumes values. It chooses a value to be ideal in regards of the importance accorded to the will, and we can easily see that the personality is largely our own work – the fruit of our persevering efforts and a progressive conquest.

Mankind has constantly struggled to defend him/herself against our enemies – both external and internal ones. Among the fiercest enemies are the routines that tend to mechanize us, and our passions, which tend to enchain and confine us. The environment tends to depersonalize us and in fact, make us functionally, its tool. Our personality is in a permanent state of becoming; it is constantly and unceasingly experiencing reconstruction. The crucial role in the formation of the personality belongs to purely psychological factors.

Personality, Character, and Fate

For Arthur Schopenhauer, a German philosopher, our destiny is determined by our immutable character. This fatalistic idea drives us to pessimism and causes us to no longer have any chance at impacting a change in our behavior. On the other hand, if we admit with the spiritualists (such as Plato and Sartre) that personality is the result of our effort, we will be insolent towards part of the truth.

Fatalism (Schopenhauer), as well as absolute liberties (Sartre), are two attempts, which are doomed to failure. **Our freedom is not absolute but is limited by our character and liberty, which is a liberation that consists in raising us as high as possible in the direction of autonomy and wealth.**

Depending on character and individuality, the "Me" or "ego" directs the life of individuals.

It seems incontestable that the innate dispositions of an individual lead its internal evolution, but the invisible personal feelings (which cannot be defeated) of freedom protests (such implacable determinism of character) forces us to disregard any notion of character, which, thereby, constitutes a form of fatality. Moreover, experience teaches us that certain elements of our individuality are fluid and modifiable as well as that the character presents a certain margin of malleability. There are also sharp changes brought about by age, by the profession, and by the environment.

The personality leaves nothing that belongs to his/her life, external to the individual. It constitutes a synthesis, and it forms the concrete totality of the "ego," whose character constitutes a sort of sub-nature. It is, therefore, the free and self-conscious "Me" that realizes the reconciliation of the diverse elements. Owing to this, mankind no longer appears as a machine launched by a necessary mechanism or as a passive and irresponsible instrument of a blind destiny. It is what requires us, as an individual, to master our will, and our destiny within a situation of which it must understand and appreciate the circumstances, consequences, and possibilities.

Mankind has the chance to become a new person at any

moment, richer and sincerer, and where we can remedy the unknowns of our character. Our destiny is to accept or reject what our individual character proposes and it is a fascinating field for the activity and exercising of our free will. It will not completely change the character but it will find within the framework of each character, infinite possibilities of functioning, spiritual evolutions, and happiness.

CHAPTER 19:

EGO : MY ADVERSARY

EGO

| #14: THE EGO |

Having detailed all the aspects of the psyche to emphasize their important role in the profound unity expressed in our identity as an ego, we unraveled the power of our psychic life (and its influences on our daily functions). Therefore, undeniably the ego and our subconscious are directing the movie of our life, and have managed to pull the biggest deception of our time. It hides and exists in every possible place, it talks to us in the first person so we think it is "us," and it will slip in whenever the opportunity arises to set you up for a challenge.

It is important to recognize that the ego is not who you really are; you are first a soul, then a body with an ego. As elaborated previously, the ego is all that you have acquired to fit in. Therefore, this survival tool only cares about itself and its own survival, especially its momentary pleasures.

To demonstrate how our ego leads us to act subconsciously and impulsively, let me tell you a story: On a beautiful sunny day in Paris, a man sat in a beautiful café, enjoying his morning coffee as he read the newspaper. Somebody rushed towards him and screamed, "Michael, I have just seen your wife cheating on you with another man!" Hearing this, the man rushed to the kitchen, grabbed a knife, and ran out without looking to cross the boulevard. A speeding car passed and hit him. The ambulance arrived and took him to the hospital when he woke up in total shock. He started to think that he needed to take control over his own life, after all he said, "My name is not Michael and I am not married!"

The ego is invisible, which makes it very difficult to understand. Throughout our human history, our own egos have managed to create the biggest deceptions in our lives. They have convinced people of some kind of an evil entity that wears red, has horns and lives in a sea of fire… all so they can project their negative aspects towards something external and separate from them. **Isn't that a human nature, where we find it easier and way more comfortable to blame someone or something else?**

Evil is not what most people believe it is!

Can you tell me who does evil in the world? Do we see a being (the devil) dressed in a red suit and horns precipitating the evil?

In fact, is it not the human beings, who make a choice inclined towards evil? So why are we blaming a devil? Where is our sense of responsibility towards our actions and accountability towards our own evil inclinations? As a matter of fact, there is power when taking responsibility of the totality of ourselves, as it liberates us from the illusion the ego wants us under, because we then recognize that we can actually do something about it.

In Judaism, one of the things Jews struggle against every day is the "evil inclination," also known as the yetzer hara (עֵרָה רֶצֵי, from Genesis 6:5). The yetzer hara is neither a being nor an angel that defied God. It is the congenital inclination to do evil, by violating the will of God; it is mankind's innate capacity for doing evil in the world. In the story of the creation in both the Torah and the Quran, when God announced to the angels the creation of mankind, they asked God, "Why are you placing on earth someone who would spread mischief?" God replied, **"I know what you do not know."** What could this have meant? Aren't we (mankind) the only ones that are bringing and allowing evil into this world? Who can stand against the all-powerful Creator?

Correspondingly, the devil (or "Ha-Satan") is an almost perfect stunt, which has been invented by the ego. It was easy to create such a character, as it continues to camouflage the job of the ego, which is to pose as our antagonist and oppose us in every aspect of our lives.

More than 3,000 years ago, according to Jewish and Christian traditions Moses wrote the original Hebrew Bible, the Torah. Therefore, if we need to find the traces of birth of this character called "the devil," it should be somewhere in this book, which is also known as the Old Testament. On extensive review, what we come to find, from time to time, are passages of a figure that is called "Ha-Satan," who is one of the angels in the heavenly court and one of God's servants. This Satan has no power on his own and does only what God commands him to do. In the entire Old Testament, we find no evidence of a story of a prince of darkness and no concept at all of an evil angel. If we study the Hebrew Bible, and as well, the Quran, we can see that angels are God's creations too, and they are celestial beings, who, unlike mankind are not endowed with the free will to make their own decisions. Instead, they are created, performing God's bestowed functions. **Therefore, how can we explain an angel created by God, but capable of defying Him?**

Satan and the Story of Job

One of the famous stories of the Bible that references Satan and his job with mankind also mentions the most faithful man of God and his expression of the deep love that mankind are capable of revealing toward the Creator. It also talks about mankind's longing for the divine... as without Him, our entire existence would simply not exist. Blessed be He.

This story, as told in Job 1:22, talked about a man named Job who lived in the land of Uz. He was one of the richest men on earth with a very large family of seven sons and three daughters. Job was not an Israelite, he had no family tree, and all the things that happened to him did not take place in the Promised Land. He was not a member of the old covenant community, but, like Noah, he had a personal covenantal relationship with the Lord. Job had not committed any sin – it was said by God himself in the text, "He is blameless and upright, a man who fears God and shuns evil" (v. 8). And so God called Job "my servant" (v. 8). This very significant phrase in the Old Testament thus indicates his especially close and deep relationship with the Creator. When the day came where all the heavenly beings appeared before the Creator, Satan was amongst them. God asked him, "What have you been doing?" Satan answered, "I have been walking here and there, roaming around the earth." And so "Did you notice my servant Job?" God asked. "There is no one on earth as faithful and good as he is. He worships me and is careful not to do anything evil." Then Satan replied, "Would Job worship you if he got nothing out of it? (v. 10) you have always protected him and his family and everything he owns. You bless everything he does, and you have given him enough cattle to fill the whole country. (v. 11) But now, suppose you take away everything he has – he will curse you to your face!" "All right," God said to Satan, "everything he has is in your power, but you must not hurt Job himself." And so then Satan left to do his job.

Despite losing his entire wealth, receiving the message about the death of all his children and all the health difficulties inflicted upon him, Job stood up and tore his clothes in grief. He shaved his head and threw himself face downwards on the ground. He said, "I was born with nothing, and I will die with nothing. The LORD gave, and now he has taken away. May his name be praised!" At this very moment, Satan lost the argument that he made in front of God.

It is well evident that Satan, who made Job's life a misery, is neither a bad angel nor lives in hell. We do not find evidence in the Old Testament of any concept of hell or the devil in its current form. Where is the Satan who lives in hell that most people know about? Where is the monster that rules over hell and the fallen angels, the legion of helpers tempting people so they can win their soul? So, if this doesn't come from the Old Testament where then does it come from?

Research of When and Where the Word With the Concept of "Hell" Appeared

Research clearly evidences that the actual word "hell" doesn't appear in the language until approximately AD 725. In addition, it doesn't come from the Hebrew language but, according to the Barnhart Concise Dictionary of Etymology, it is ultimately rooted in Proto-Germanic. In fact, it is derived from the word "helan," which also has been spelled "hele," "helle," "hell," and "heile." In its original form, it simply meant, "to cover, conceal, and hide."

The word "hell" was adopted into the current vocabulary with the object to introduce the pagan concept of hell into Christian theology. The Gospel's passage where Yeshua (Christ) used the word "hell" in Greek, it is "γέεννα" (Gehenna), which actually means "The Valley of the

Son of Hinnom." Gehenna is a small valley in Jerusalem, which was used as the garbage dump outside the city – the location can be traced way back to the book of Joshua, and this place was known for the happenings of unpleasant and dreadful things. The garbage and dead bodies would be discarded, at this place and consumed by a fire that was most likely always burning. According to the scriptures, the king of Judah sacrificed his children there by fire. Thereafter, the valley was deemed to be cursed. However, this was a very literal place and the audience of Yeshua would have heard the word "Gehenna" and understood its reference to an actual place outside the city of Jerusalem. With this knowledge, they would not have conceived of the place as we do, in our current concept of hell.

About 3,500 years ago in ancient Persia where Syria, Iraq, and Iran are today, there were several gods – good and evil ones. Then a man called Zoroaster appeared, who was an ancient Iranian-speaking prophet. His teachings and innovations on the religious traditions of ancient Iranian-speaking people became the religion of Zoroastrianism, which (by some accounts) was the first world religion. He taught that dual opposing forces emanate from the all-one God who created the world and these dual forces are in continual equal cosmic battle. This dualism stems from the nature of the Creator and not of the universe. Correspondingly, Ahura Mazda referred to the good absolute power and Angra Mainyu referred to the evil forces that are not at all powerful. **According to Zoroaster, mankind – both women and men – are born pure and sinless and can choose from good or evil.** Mankind's ultimate destiny is the exercise of our free will to choose between these two. He believed that mankind played an essential role in the struggle of the forces of good and evil in the universe.

Over time, Gehenna, developed beyond the name of a place; the term came to stand for something supernatural and a spiritual faith that awaits people after death. Subsequently, when the Christians Gospels were written towards the end of the 1st century AD, Satan had, in fact, grown into a powerful figure. This emergence of Satan was during the time when the Roman Empire reigned and many Jews and Christians were persecuted. Later on, in the Book of Revelations, the writer accords Satan an interesting name: "the beast." The beast can refer to the Emperor Nero Caesar of that time. It was also mentioned that "the beast" has a human number – 666. Likewise, if we count the numeric value in Aramaic for Nero Caesar (רסק ןורנ NRON QSR), of which its numbers represent 50 200 6 50 100 60 200, we can see that they add up to 666.

Are you surprised yet on how the human ego works?

So, What is Hell?

The most practical representation of hell can be described as the psychological states, intentions, and thoughts, which stem from holding on to various forms of negativity. In other words, it refers to all our evil inclinations, which we failed to overcome: Such as pride, hate, selfishness, irrational fear, anger, arrogance, greed, lust, envy, doubt, and the other possible forms of evil inclinations.

Essentially, all afterlife experiences are the energetic dimensions of our own personal consciousness, as they form a part of our present life experiences. They transpire within our more subtle inner dimensions of consciousness and can be considered similar to our experiences of dreams. Only these dreams states are said to be a hundred times more powerful than our strongest human dreams and significantly more vivid and intense. Because our bodies have experienced the biological death, we no longer maintain the ability to exit these dimensions by returning to our body and restoring ourselves to waking consciousness. Meanwhile, this experience can sustain for a very long time, in fact, until we are permitted to pass into another incarnation – and whether we are experiencing a heavenly or hellish realm, or maybe something in between.

As the concept of time (as we know it in this reality) does not exist on the other side, one second there may feel like an eternity. **It is said that the moment our consciousness leaves the body, the soul feels all the thoughts, emotions, words, negativity, deeds, mischief, and more, in one particular moment.** A hellish realm would not be even close to being suspended as a human in the midst of a heavy thunderstorm where the roars of the thunder are an assault on the hearing and the lightning will nearly blind the visual senses, and where this situation has no end. That is exactly what most prophets have talked about when referring to the hell or Gehenna. However, it is logical that no humans would be alive today if we experienced the consequences of our actions, all at once. Therefore, in what state of consciousness do you desire to leave this embodiment? Would you even want to leave your embodiment prior to do the work of looking inwards at your states of consciousness when you become aware that you will face in the afterlife realms that match the mental and vital energy created by you in this particular life? Rather, these experiences of the afterlife will be increasingly more heightened, more powerful and more real than even this physical dimension! Because they will last until the mental and vital energy behind them is exhausted, the karmic continuum thus plays itself out, easily making eternity feel short.

Evidently, there is, indeed, a judgment... although it is not the Creator that is inflicting it on mankind. As we have just detailed, we are the creators of judgment. Would you be able to imagine what it means to love, totally unconditionally and infinitely, while simultaneously feeling absolutely no attachments to the physical matter? This is exactly one of the aspects of being like the Creator. Mankind has forgotten that Love can indeed do miracles, which is indeed the most extraordinary manifestations of Love. A very important precondition of creation was set by the Divine as one of the most important laws of our universe: Irrespective of how far or deep a soul travels into the darkness, **there will forever be a way to come back.** Thus, in reality, each one of us, is creating our own judgment for the afterlife, and all this is happening internally or subconsciously. We exist in a universe that follows divine and natural laws where anything that goes against these laws violates the very essence of their existence.

But, there will be too a Divine judgment that will come upon all living creatures, however, this day will happen only in the Divine's time. What kind of an egocentric state would lead someone to think that mankind has the utmost full right to judge and penalize his/her own people, using the legal system established by mankind? And even in some parts of the world, where they still have the capital penalty for certain crimes, doesn't the Divine Creator of the entire universe has the right to govern it? I can already hear your ego defense saying, "What nonsense is that?" But just as our human world needs order, so does the Divine world. But, then you say, "The Divine is only good."

Yes! Indeed, it is only good. And good is what the Creator holds and wants for us to choose. But how many of us still choose evil? Yes! Too many do!

Why? For several reasons, but primarily all these actions are underpinned by our egocentricity, and we deny all what the Creator perpetually does for us. Each time you choose to satisfy your evil inclinations (greed, hate, judgments, abuse of self and others, and any negative trait whether you are aware of it or not); your actions impact major consequences in the non-physical plane. Just because, the naked human eye, fails to perceive the actual energetic effect of your own thoughts and actions, it doesn't mean they are not real. As humans, we don't see the tons of data flying through the sky and around you at all time, whizzing into your mobile or computer to appear on your screen either. However, do you doubt the existence of this wireless invisible quantum field of information exchange? Likely, you firmly believe in the technology, although you probably (like so many of us) are unaware of how it exactly works. But you still believe it exists. Therefore, why are you denying yourself the expansion of your own consciousness to possibilities? There is a significant passage in Psalms 119:1 that says, "Praiseworthy are those whose way is perfect, who walk with the law of the Lord." By "perfect," it refers to following "good." Thus, what may seem to you as a judgment from your physical perspective, it is merely a call to Light your way out of the darkness. Which is represented by this verse, "I shall thank You with an upright heart, when I know the judgments of Your righteousness." (Psalms 119:7)

We have inherited the most precious gift: "Free Will." Eliphas Levi, a French occult author, once said that by **"Freedom (free will), one might call the Divinity of Humanity. It is the most beautiful, the most superb, the most irrevocable of all of the Creator's gifts to us. The Supreme Creator will not violate this Freedom without denying its own nature."**

Thus, the nature of this afterlife judgment is sourced from the universal law of "cause and effect" based on our individual choices, and choice exists as a by-product of our inherited free will. Therefore, we constitute the deciding factors by each conscious or subconscious decision, thought, action, emotion, etc. Furthermore, our own intentions, whether they are good or bad, ability or inability to let go of self-judgment, to forgive and be forgiven, hate or love, kindles or unkindness, greed or sharing, and whether we have the innate desire to receive only for the self. They will all act as a catalyst for our judgment in the afterlife.

One could say that the afterlife experiences are the

unwinding of the accumulated psychic tension that binds the soul. The fascinating representation of the afterlife passage is evident in the preserved papyrus of the Last Judgment day in the Book of the Dead of Ancient Egypt. The Book of the Dead is a funerary text of spells, drafted with the objective to assist the deceased in their journey through the afterlife. This papyrus is exhibited at the British Museum in London and shows us, using symbolism, how our hearts will individually be weighed against a feather on the judgment day. And, should the feather prevail, the monster will eat the soul. Alternatively, we access the heavenly realms and continue our journey of development, evolution, and service to others.

Therefore, hell is something we make for ourselves, it is of our own choosing, out of the decisions and choices we make in life. It is created for us individually as an outcome of our state of consciousness, as a result of living subconsciously through our conditioned and programmed mind, as well out of allowing our egos to take control over our actions and lives. Thus, the concept of hell is uniquely personal and individual to each of the 7.4 billion humans on earth.

The Power of Ego

Our egos exercise this invisible power over us that hides from our sight, consciousness, and awareness (which we can call our blind spots). It sustains constant conversations with us, without taking any rest, and it talk to us in the first person, so we believe it is us. However, mankind has apparently grown comfortable with blaming everything bad on something external to us. In fact, as discussed earlier, everything happens and is sourced internally. This illusion which has been created by the ego has kept people focused on the effects and not on the cause of our actions. Although make no mistake, evil is very real and does exist – it is an energy that is within us.

It is with us from birth, surrounding us all the time, and it lays waiting, at every opportunity, to set us up. Herein, it is our job to strengthen our self-awareness, as darkness is a consequence and the representation of the absence of light. Whenever people distance themselves from the Creator, the darkness fills their beings, rendering them oblivious, fueling their egoistic and evil inclinations that easily overpower them. If you believe in creation in which everything has been created by the Divine, in that case, everything is a part of this Divine. Therefore, this ego, too, should be considered and perceived as a gift from the Creator, who bestowed upon it the job to challenge us so we can exercise, our most and utter precious gift, i.e. our "free will."

With our free will, we can earn, receive, and invite the Light in our lives through the choices we make. To achieve this transition, we need to resist our reactions as they come out of our ego. Whenever you resist, you are altering the process of projecting your "id" externally and thus taking a moment to allow your true self, your soul, to shine through. When we are faced with situations (especially the ones that threatens us), out of fear, the ego makes us react in three ways: fight, flight, or freeze. These reactions will be discussed more in-depth later in the chapter. These situations (or even people) are in fact, due to our conditioning perceived as threats, and therefore rejected or removed. However, although these situations don't fit within our ego system, they do fit within our soul. Due to the polarity of life – good and bad – we need to experience them, so we can accord ourselves a fair choice and recognize what we are not. The most difficult step in any challenging situation is to pause, which is the hardest part, and at times we are unable to help ourselves. However, we always have a choice to identify and select the forward direction for ourselves. At every single opportunity in life (bad or good, fear or love, compassion or indifference, etc.), the ego operates to let us feel that we do not have a choice. The intention of the ego here is to protect itself and not really you! In fact, if any individual continues to do what the ego only wants them to do at all time, this will lead them to self-destruction, eventually. Does this remind you the actions of anybody? Yourself, maybe?

Everything that is currently going wrong or is chaotic in my life cannot be simply blamed on my ego or the situation or any other individual, but it is purely and simply because of my reactions. When you can see the Divine spark, even within those who would mean you harm, then you perceive the big design and our individual parts in this grand drama of life, created for us to co-create, grow, assist others, and know thyself. The famous quote of Jack Sparrow in the movie *The Pirates of the Caribbean* summarizes this very well: **"The problem is not the problem, the problem is your attitude toward the problem."**

Why Does the Ego Exist?

To understand this phenomenon and answer this question, we have to go back about 15 billion years just before the big bang occurred and caused the existence of our earth. This story has been told from a Kabbalistic perspective and begins with before the creation of the universe when there was only the endless, the infinite Light that also we refer to as God. God wanted to share all His Light, which is pure love and fulfillment, but there was nobody with whom to share it with. So God decided to create a being, who could be the receiver of His Light. This being was one giant soul, which God filled with His infinite love, fulfillment, and happiness.

The vessel was only receiving, and because it had the soul DNA of God, it wanted to earn and feel the pleasure of receiving. Yet, as it had not still experienced the lack of the Light of the Creator, it was totally oblivious to the value of the gifts, it was receiving. Imagine growing up in a place where everything was handed to you without any effort, just everything you desired it was there. Would you grow appreciative of them while you never knew the notion of lack? "Unless you have bad times, you can't appreciate the good times," said American professional baseball player Joe Torre.

So the giant soul was oblivious, unaware, and subconscious to what it was receiving. This can be attributed to the fact that the soul was created in a perfect state of total fulfillment, where it was receiving everything it desired totally without any effort. (Just exactly the same way that you may have been unappreciative or oblivious towards your mother nursing you day and night at birth). At exactly that moment, something very great happened. The giant soul shattered itself and the effect caused the creation of our reality to experience all the aspects of God.

The purpose of the big bang was to create a dimension wherein the soul could experience contrasts of the Light to appreciate the blessings. Therefore, in our lives, every negative and dark aspect, which we see is the contrast of what we are not. For these reasons, we chose to experience the contrast of God, i.e. when there was unimaginable joy, there would be counter unimaginable sadness, and so on. Thus, a genuine happiness, joy, and fulfillment can only be appreciated when presented with contrast. (The contrast of love is fear, the contrast of success is a failure, etc.). Therefore, it can be inferred that for the soul to know and appreciate God, it had to experience the absence of God and the loss of the free fulfillment. It was and is the only way. The ego is, in fact, a tool for the material world, which is intended to operate as a survival mechanism, just as our intuition is on this earthly plane. It seeks competition and thrives to be the best, although, what most do not realize, due its survival function, it creates, rather fear and worry.

The Ego – Our Cunning Antagonist

"Careful with your ego, he is the one that we should blame." ~ Alicia Keys, in her song *Brand New Me*.

Are you able to identify the loud voice in your head that keeps telling that you are not good enough, you are not beautiful enough, and you are not worthy enough? Do you feel controlled by a non-ending committee discussion in your mind? This same voice pulls you out of your way by planting doubt, fear, and worry whenever you want to venture forward to do something. **That is the job of the ego, our very cunning antagonist.**

Its entire existence is based on opposing us. Relatively, in fact, it has, as well, created for itself "a devil" with a very bad reputation, since the beginning of time. This concept is deeply ingrained in humans, and to the extent that the entire human race fears it. This was clearly evident to me when once I sent a friend a picture of a book I was reading. It had the word "Satan" on it. She got perturbed, told me that this is a dangerous subject, and asked me not to discuss this matter with her. I laughed about this for few days. However, the choice is ultimately for each individual to see through the veil of illusions.

When you closely observe the ego, you will notice that everything, which it seeks to validate is an entity that is external to us. Its purpose is, indeed, what most psychologists also referred to for hundreds of years: A survival mechanism. This should be positively perceived as a powerful tool bestowed upon us by the Creator with a function to receive the pain instead of the actual soul, which is the observer. How beautiful and loving is that?

Anytime you are in a situation and you feel the urge to react, **this is your ego in action.** The more you practice being conscious, aware and proactive towards the way you behave, the stronger you'll become and enabled to master the ego's ways to oppose you. There is a wonderful reference to the ego in the bible which says, "I can of mine own self do nothing: as I hear, I judge: and my judgment is just; because I seek not mine own will, but the will of the Father which hath sent me." (John 5:30) Just after that, it says, **"If I bear witness of myself, my witness is not true."** (John 5:31)

Whenever you experience the negative emotions of feeling down, sad, unvalued, etc., remind yourself that these are a result of your ego. The lesson is to let it get the beating. When you walk into a situation and you feel embarrassed, let that feeling sink in; do not run away from it. Absorb all the variable aspects and emotional manifestations of you that don't want you to be in that situation. Stay still with it. Allow it to exist parallel in your conscious mind, and don't suppress it, so you can transform it. When you figure out the aspect of you that needs to be transformed, healed, or loved, you will be presented with the opportunity for correcting that aspect directly at its seed, from where it originates.

Our individual acquired identity is not who we really are, which is the soul. An identity is this entire conditioned construct of beliefs, habits, languages, morals, profession, food, etc. that we are born into and acquired to conform, adapt, and be accepted either in the family, at school, society, work, etc. Humans are a social race and we cannot survive individually, we thrive on the constructs of society and community. We need other beings to share and learn from.

The Most Powerful Tools the Ego Uses

Fear, it is that feeling of being in a threatening or dangerous situation and it manifests itself via many forms: worry, unease, anxiety, nervousness, tension, phobia, etc. Psychological fear is a fear of something that might happen, not of something that is happening now. The most accurate definition of fear has been given by Jean-Paul Sartre in his book *Being and Nothingness*. Sartre defined fear as occurring whenever we view our "self" as an object and no longer as "a free will being," and whenever the things around us are the ones in control of our own life, causing us to lose our sense of freedom. However, in his description, Sartre forgot to mention is that this fear originates from the inherent ego that we are born with, and anything that threatens its survival, leads to the creation of fear. Even babies can be fearful of things such as loud noises, sudden movements, and unfamiliar faces.

Once faced with fear, the ego (our survival mechanism) will make us react in three ways: fight, flight or freeze, which constitute our most primitive and powerful survival reactions. **The moment our brain perceives a threat or a dangerous situation, it commands our adrenal glands, located above our kidneys, to release bucket loads of adrenaline, which increases our heart rate, pumps blood to our muscles, and moves our attention toward a singular focus: Fighting off, getting away, or freezing!**

Our Three Reactions to Fear

Why do we fight? People who are able to see the reward in a particular situation are risk takers and often fight back, if they are aware of a chance of defeating it, or of being victorious. Note that we are not talking about, for example, facing and fighting a bear, as our natural response would be to flee because we are not equipped to battle the fierce animal.

Why do we flee (or take flight)? People who are avoidant of confrontations, or facing certain situations – especially neurotic types – tend to predominantly perceive the risks in the majority of situations as negatives. Moreover, we take flight when we are faced with something that potentially can harm us.

Why do we freeze (or even faint)? We freeze in order to buy time to assess the situation before deciding on whether to fight or flee. The length of the freeze time depends on the distance of the threat, the perceived (or real) danger, or the confronting situation. Fainting, however, is an escape mechanism from the current reality exercised by our brain in helpless circumstances and the trauma exceeds our handling capability.

This, naturally leads us to question ourselves: Why and how did we get to fear everything and we forget about the only "fear" that we should have in our life? Yeshua (Christ) in (Matthew 10:28) said, "And fear not them that kill the body, but are not able to kill the soul; but rather fear Him that is able to destroy both soul and body in hell." This metaphor is stated by Yeshua in a perspective tailored for the elevation of consciousness to his audience. It conveys a deeper, loving message that we should only "fear" to lose the connection with the Divine who created mankind out of Love for sharing, and which perpetually sustains the entire cosmos for us to live. Without the Divine Light and blessings, everything would cease to exist.

Now, imagine instead if Yeshua would have told his audience: You need to fear to lose the connection with the Light of God who created and continues to sustain this entire cosmos. Definitely, such a convenient message would have simply passed way over their heads and failed to draw the tiniest bit of their attention. Thousands of years ago, various spiritual enlightenment knowledge, wisdom, or scientific concepts were neither welcomed nor comprehensible by the majority of people. At that time even the forecast of planes or mobile phones would have resulted in the burning of the forecaster at the stake, branding them as witches. **Yet, all of this did happen!**

There is a beautiful Surat (text) in the Quran, called "Al-Rahman," which also discusses this subject. The Arabic word "Al Rahman" translates to "The Beneficent." In this section of text, the prophet discusses all the blessings the Creator has given mankind and asked 31 times, "So which of the favors of your Lord would you deny?" **The majority of people still deny that all that exists is sustained only because the Creator allows it to exist.**

How Can You Manage or Decrease the Perception of Fear?

You can manage or decrease the perception of fear by understanding you are a free will being with a birthright to freedom. These varied freedoms include physical, mental, emotional, and spiritual freedom, and your free will is inherently involved in the ability to express itself at any time without restrictions. However, depending on our belief system or the strength of the ego stronghold on us, freedom can take on different forms. For example, if we believe that we are subjects and part of nature, we are bound by its laws. And if we believe that there is a Divine realm, then we are subject to its laws. Thus, in turn, our task is to find out what these laws are and abide by them. **Both of these principles are instinctively frustrating to mankind.**

Our free will is bound to our desires and, therefore, ultimately its exercise depends on the nature of our individual culture, society, environment, and other associated factors. This entire universe thrives on maintaining balance up to the atomic level of this reality. Thus, it is always a two-way street of exchange for all matter, energies, frequencies, and vibrations. However, by learning about and understanding the laws that govern the universe, we can further manage or decrease our perception of fear.

The 12 Universal Laws

The Law of Divine Oneness: As discussed previously, we all comprise from the same atoms and, therefore, everything is connected to everything, creating a unity of "oneness." Furthermore, everything we say, act, think, and believe, in turn, affects others and the surrounding universe irrespective of the individual visibility.

The Law of Vibration: This law states that everything in the universe vibrates, moves, and oscillates in circular patterns. This includes each type of matter, sound, and even though it has its own vibrational frequency, unique to each of them.

The Law of Action: Nothing remains still in the universe, therefore, this law must be applied in order for matter to manifest things on earth, such as our thoughts dreams, emotions, and desires.

The Law of Correspondence: This law states that the principles or laws of physics that explain the physical world of energy, light, vibration, and motion have their corresponding principles in the etheric universe. "As above, so below." (Matthew 6: 9-13)

The Law of Cause and Effect: Nothing happens randomly in our universe. Every action has an equal and opposite reaction or consequence, which can be summarized by the famous proverb "We reap what we sow."

The Law of Compensation: This law of cause and effect applies to blessings and abundance that are provided for us. The visible effects of our deeds are given to us in gifts, fulfillment, happiness, equanimity, friendships, etc.

The Law of Attraction and Repulsion: This law demonstrates how our thoughts, feelings, words, and actions produce energies, which, in turn, attract like symbiotic energies. Attraction is one of two forces contained within magnetism. The other is repulsion. Magnetism does not operate without both poles.

The Law of Perpetual Transmutation of Energy: We are all equipped with the power to change our lives at any moment. Even if an individual went very deep into the darkest psychic states of being, there is always a way back through redemption. When we invite the Divine into our lives, His Light will extinguish the darkness.

The Law of Relativity: This law assists us in our physical reality by giving us a series of tests as lessons for the purpose of strengthening the light and consciousness within each one of us. It allows us to mirror others so we can compare our problems and orient them into their proper perspectives. Through this law, each individual receives the designated lessons to nudge them towards fulfillment.

The Law of Polarity: Everything in our physical reality is on a continuum path and presents an opposite. We can transform undesirable thoughts by concentrating on the opposite polarity. It is the law of mental vibrations that operates along the law of cause and effect to reveal for us the consequences of our actions or decisions.

The Law of Rhythm: Everything vibrates and moves to certain rhythms. These rhythms establish in our physical and non-physical reality the seasons, cycles, stages of development, and patterns.

The Law of Gender: This is the law that governs what we know as creation. The law of gender manifests in all things biological as masculine and feminine.

My Ego is my Ally and it is Here to Stay!

In the Garden of Eden, Adam and Eve were in a state of receiving everything effortlessly and without asking. The Creator is in an eternal state of giving, although, back then, we were oblivious to what we were receiving, as we were created in the perfect state of fulfillment. Therefore, we demanded these conditions in our physical reality, and one of these conditions is for our ego to exist as our challenger in life. **Imagine if nothing challenged or motivated us to grow? We would never lift a finger!** These conditions are merely the effect of the cause of our desire to reveal the light of God through the darkness in the physical dimension. It was and is the only way as shall be always. Therefore, the only thing that stands between us and God's Light is allowing our "self" to be mastered by the ego, instead of us mastering and gaining control of this fascinating tool.

CHAPTER 20:

NO PAIN, NO GAIN

It has been observed that while few individuals understand clearly the principle: **The greater the pain, the bigger the gain.** For others, however, mottos like "no pain, no gain" don't really imply much and neither do they acknowledge the principle. However, they need to think again!

"No pain, no gain" is the promise of a greater reward for the price of hard and maybe even painful work. Consider: Can you become a successful athlete without daily hours of extensive exercising or practice? (I spent years avoiding the gym and use wishful thinking that my genes would simply grow me nice muscles. Guess what? This never happened until I dragged myself to the gym). Can you evolve to become every day a better version of you without doing any of the internal work required?

The imminent answer to all of such questions is a big and shiny "No!"

However, if you have answered, "Yes," then you are living in denial. Becoming consciously self-aware is not an easy or comfortable process. It doesn't feel good to acknowledge or recognize things about ourselves that we don't want to see, nor does it feel good to recognize truths that we don't want to be true. This is especially true if your emotional self remains a child and does not change, irrespective of the achievement of individual enlightenment. We can either learn how to better parent our emotional selves or learn to build an armor of protection around us.

It is logical that an individual would be unable to evolve, learn, grow, and acquire a goal, simply by sitting comfortably on the sofa or bed while wishfully thinking that things will just fall into their lap. Being in a still state without progression is in contradiction with the human nature, and it's not how natural laws operate. Even wisdom would not be real wisdom if it is confined to just reading it from books without embodying, practicing, and living it in our daily lives. For example, just like the sun that keeps on shining every day and every second, whether you see it or not. It perpetually gives its light to Earth without prejudice, discrimination, or any disruption. Its entire purpose is to forever shine its light upon earth to sustain life.

Time as a Linear Continuum

American artist and author Jose Arguelles (A.K.A. Valum Votan) once said, **"Who owns your time owns your mind; own your own time and know your own mind."**

The idea of time existed way before the clocks were invented. Though the first instance when the time was recorded is under debate, the first standard time was adopted on December 1st, 1847, with the adoption of Greenwich Mean Time (also called Railway Time). Time inexorably moves forward and time's progression is embodied in our perceptions of the linear continuum of our experiences to recognize the present, the past, and the future. It allows us to progress, learn, gain, recognize, rectify, evolve, and more. **In fact, it would be impossible to discuss and review the imperative functions of motion or dynamics without the concept of time and its progression.**

However, in the early twentieth century, Einstein, in his theory of relativity, found that space and time were not separate, but rather intersecting concepts, which were interwoven together as a single, united continuum: Scientists refer to the same as "space-time." It is also important to add that time is not linear, as we are taught to believe. In the third dimension, it appears to be so, but this is yet another illusion of our reality, as all times exist simultaneously. **Everything is a big NOW** and happening at the same time, and hence there is no past and there is no future. It is quite frustrating for a linear brain to grasp a nonlinear concept. Eckhart Tolle describes this perfectly in his book *The Power of Now*.

Without the existence of space-time, no human beings would be alive today. Should time banish every single action, thought, intention, feeling, emotion; these human phenomena will instantly boomerang to each one of us, as we would be its source. There is no way anybody can handle and survive the physical reality without the concept of space-time.

Mankind: L'Uomo Vitruviano

As newborns, we are clean slates, empty canvases that we fill in with the experiences of life… just like an empty hard disk or memory bank that you fill in bit by bit with tons of information. Therefore, this question is directed to parents: What kind of experiences would you like your child to acquire and record that will influence his/her entire life?

The human body is an entire universe in it is own. It is a vehicle of perfection. Leonardo Da Vinci's drawing, "The Vitruvian Man" (also called "L'Uomo Vitruviano"), details the proportions of the human body. We find the golden ratio in these divine proportions of the body. The human body is based on patterns of 5, which is as well the basis for Phi (the symbol for the golden ratio is the Greek letter "phi"). The golden ratio (also called the golden number or golden mean, is the rounded number 1.618, which equals 5 to the exponent 0.5 multiplied by 0.5 plus 5, or "5 ^ .5 x .5 + .5."

The observation of nature and the expression of the golden number alongside the vector patterns like the sunflower seeds or Romanesco broccoli, reveals that these beautiful foods are also mathematical marvels. The pattern evident within them follows the Fibonacci sequence, which is the pattern 1, 2, 3, 5, 8, 13... etc. Each number in this sequence is the sum of the previous two numbers. Their spirals are generated using this sequence. Trees even follow this sequence to allow balance when growing branches. Science now is discussing how trees and vegetation can even communicate with each other using an underground network.

The ancient Egyptians knew of our existence as spiritual beings living an earthly experience and this idea underpinned their life philosophy of spending majority of their lives with the concern of being able to access the afterlife. They dedicated their entire existence to worshiping their gods and goddesses to ask help in the passage through the spiritual realms. Pyramids were built using the golden ratio, too.

Today's civilizations spend most of their lives worried about earthly things, forgetting that we are, as well, souls. We have created an organized system that restricts space for spirituality. However, notably, I don't in this instance mean the current form of religions. The majority of religions, in their present format, do not offer the right tools for people to become awakened to their individual consciousness. Humanity went through the Age of Enlightenment in the middle of the 17th century and wanted to find scientific evidence or a theory for pretty much everything that constitutes our universe. Scientists even challenged all the existing doctrines and dogmas. The ripple effect of this enlightenment phase did not serve humanity in the bigger scheme of things. Rather, it put us on the path of the spiritual Dark Age. Science is unable to explain various earthly subjects, too, such as why it takes more genes to make a tomato than a human, how the placebo effect actually works, and how the impossibly energetic cosmic rays come to Earth. Moreover, it is not able to understand the functionality of our brain, or yet the focal residence of our consciousness. Correspondingly, even our medical system has not encountered optimal success in treating chronic diseases or finding cures for them (such as cancer), despite the continued efforts.

Several people who have died and come back to life, talk about feeling a mystical experience the moment they left their bodies. We are eternal souls, and this part of us, which can never die, is thus also something no one can harm. We all have out-of-body experiences every night when we sleep. However, few people are able to recall the experience. Dreams are communications from within us. Jung frequently discussed how we dream in archetypical ways. That's how our soul communicates with us – in subtle ways – and because we have not learned that language, we do not know how to interpret our dreams.

How can we go through life solely living one aspect of us – the mind-body – and ignore the soul? Why do we spend hours at the hair salon, at the gym, or shopping, and fail to even spend 15 minutes each day being grateful to the Highest who created our entire existence? We fail to realize the imperative nature of catering to the needs of the soul. Thus, in order to have a complete and fulfilling experience, we must cater to both of our aspects – the mind-body and the soul. For the believers in prayers; prayers are the desires that you wish into existence and with a focus of your energy, the universe manifests (for you) the same.

For thousands of years now, with the aimless progression, humanity has forgotten who we are as a race and has lost its way and purpose. With time, we fell into a Dark Age of materialism, emotional denial, and abuse of the self, others, animals, and even nature. In fact, we have allowed the ego to get away with dominating and controlling us and directing our lives. We have lived for too long; ruled by this powerful antagonist without any quantifiable or tangible clue of what is really going on. This is despite the warnings of life, in the form of throwing a couple of pebbles at us. And when we don't listen to the sounds of these pebbles hitting us, inevitably we feel the brick that follows.

The ego's greed for power and control is not a new concept and can be traced back to thousands of years ago, to the Ancient Egyptian civilization, were pharaohs buried with them the Book of the Dead as well as their most precious items. At that period of time, the priest's egos saw an opportunity with this revelation and promoted receiving money from wealthy individuals to write for them the Book of the Dead, which was solely destined for pharaohs. Can you imagine the desire of how many people would have wanted to put their hands on such a book? Are you able to now identify the ways and patterns the ego utilizes to challenge you away from your path back to fulfillment?

Consequently, these egoistic choices continue to disconnect mankind from our intuition and weaken the connection to our inner being — that inner voice of knowingness that provides you with the most accurate compass to your life. As a race, we continue to drift away from the Creator, by allowing science to convince humanity of the random evolution. We also believe that we are outside of our universe on a lonely Earth in a lonely galaxy, thus magnifying the perception of how much we are separate and lonely. This is the biggest fundamental mistake that still fashions people's views of the world and themselves. It is imperative to start realizing that these views of separateness are the most destructive and harmful to us and in fact, constitute the ultimate root of all the problems in our world. This paradigm is wrong and at the very essence, we are all friends and one big family.

With each attack of humans on other humans, it seems to shatter a layer and expose our collective subconsciousness. Yet, underneath the rubble of this long-fought cold war on earth, our home, there is a deep inner truth to those attacks in this physical world. In order for the old ways to fall apart, we have to watch it decline into disorder and chaos.

Because we feel separate, we turn our eyes away from the people starving on the streets as we walk by. We turn a blind eye to people dying in other parts of the world, and to the ruthless slaughtering ways and torture of animals; some for the purpose of eating a steak or a burger, and some simply because humans are capable of being cruel.

As a species, humans show incredible adaptation abilities. Throughout centuries, we have expertly handled every revolution, war, and crisis, however, this exact strength is also our weakness. Just because we live in a system, which is a manifestation of our states of consciousness and caving into our egoistic nature does not mean this is the only solution. Each one of us is individually responsible for the repercussions of our actions and thus we are the only ones capable of transforming this current egocentric system. This, in turn, can stop the feeding of our ego where we inevitably become its master and not vice versa.

However, every change has to be initiated from within, for the successful execution and implementation of the change. We have to stop pointing fingers outward and begin dealing with our own individual evil inclinations, darkness, or the subconscious issues. Only, then would we be able to overcome these adverse aspects. It is not possible to understand others if you cannot understand yourself. We need to stop living in denial and initiate by opening our eyes to the current scenario of our own inner lives and subsequently look outwards, to the reflection of who we are.

The majority of people present major resistance to perceive the truth because of their conditioned corrupt minds. Those who have such corrupt brains and egocentrism are called people of the reprobate minds. It is mentioned in the Epistle of Paul, to Titus (one of the three

Pastoral Epistles in the New Testament), that the reprobates are those whom "profess that they know God; but in works they deny him, being abominable, and disobedient, and unto every good work reprobate." (Titus 1:16) Therefore, these are people with very little desire to please the Creator and they are in total oblivion to the desires of love and fulfillment the Creator hold for them. Most importantly, they are unable to consciously perceive that the only obstacle between them and the Creator is only themselves or their own ego.

The brewing of all the energies of negativity caused throughout centuries by mankind is not going to disappear; it will continue to transform and recycle itself. It is the most basic property of our universe: nothing disappears, but everything transforms. We will ultimately be faced with two choices: Either we can wake up through manageable pain via a spiritual growth or we can do it through suffering, ugly, and horrific external events.

Carl Jung once said, **"There is no coming to consciousness without pain. People will do anything, no matter how absurd, in order to avoid facing their own Soul. One does not become enlightened by imagining figures of light, but by making the darkness conscious."**

What would be YOUR choice between these two options?

CHAPTER 21:

DUALITY, ENERGY, FREQUENCIES, VIBRATIONS, AND ELEMENTS

"If you want to find the secrets of the universe, think in terms of energy, frequency, and vibration," said the Serbian-American inventor Nikola Tesla.

The physical reality, which we inhabit is built on those principles and designed to disguise its true essence and play hide-and-seek with us. Often, scientists discover a law explaining a theory and then, years later, we are in for another revelation when something controversial or contradictory replaces it. Are you able to perceive the chase for a very evasive, shadow-like truth that is seemingly endless? The Universe does not only disguise its real face, but it actually turns into whatever our collective consciousness and subconsciousness need it to be. That's why we call it a "mirroring universe."

What is Duality?

For thousands of years, mankind has understood that the world has a dual nature. For everything in life, there is polarity – a positive and a negative, or an opposite. Thus, to which side we connect with, in any given situation is ultimately our own choice. On the one hand, all that exists in our physical reality (such as the concept of duality) is quite comprehensible to the mind and can be explained using the natural sciences. On the other hand, the mind enters into a great frustration when faced with phenomena belonging to the metaphysical, "non-material" dimension (which operates on completely different rules than matter, which will be elaborated on next).

The mind will almost always naturally react in rejection when faced with a new event, idea, thought, or more, particularly, when it doesn't fit within the concept that it created. This is simply the way our brains work. Knowing this fact, it has to be the other way around going forward. Whenever your mind shows its ultimate dissatisfaction or when you encounter deviations of scenarios in your life that get manifested as complaining, bragging, anger, gossiping, judging, etc., you should consider it as a red flag to seek the answer to what is good for you in these changes or differences of ideas for your ego to act in such an opposing way to them. It is absolutely true that what we see as negative in the world is merely a reflection of our internal world. **Remember, we live in a mirroring universe!**

What is Energy?

It is one of the most basic concepts in physics, and also one of the hardest to define. Energy exists in different forms: light energy, heat energy, mechanical energy, sound energy, electrical energy, chemical energy, atomic or nuclear energy, etc. Scientists who studied energy, explain it as "work," which is the action of moving something against a force. But isn't this definition a bit unsatisfying?

The reason why it is so hard to define energy is due to its abstract nature. Energy, always needs a carrier or a mode of transport, usually in the form of movement. Therefore, there is no physical essence of energy and no such thing as completely pure energy. According to the Big Bang Theory, elaborated from a spiritual perspective in the introduction of the book and further in chapter 19, the present universe is a result of the unrestricted expansion of an infinite amount of energy. Thereafter, energy cooled as it had expanded and while cooling down, the particles were able to fuse together and form matter. Furthermore, scientists add that our universe is a closed system, which means that all the energy contained in the universe remains the same and simply gets exchanged or transformed. Energy can travel in the form of electromagnetic waves, such as light, heat, radio, and gamma rays. Moreover, according to the law of conservation of energy (in physics), energy can neither be created nor destroyed; rather, it can only be transformed from one form to another.

The human body produces enough energy to power a light bulb. So where does this energy go when we die? In death, this energy, which originated during the Big Bang, will always be around. Therefore, your "Light" (the essence and origin of your energy) is not to be confused with your actual consciousness; it will continue to perpetually exist throughout the universe.

What is Consciousness?

What is its Relation to Intuition?

The concept of consciousness has been explained in Chapter 4 from a psychological perspective and discussed its metaphysical repercussions. Despite the evident difficulties in defining consciousness, which is the awareness of oneself and external objects, many philosophers believed that there was a broadly-shared, underlying intuition about the nature of consciousness. To demonstrate this, move your awareness-consciousness towards the tip of your index finger on your left hand, now move it again towards the index finger on your right hand. Can you describe or explain the mechanism of how this awareness-consciousness moved towards your first finger and then the other?

In Chapter 1, we defined intuition as a kind of "empathy," wherein one tries to access the very heart of an object to coincide with it, and that coincidence is a direct contact. Intuition is, therefore, a direct grasp of the inner life – a direct vision of the mind by the mind, which is subjective and singular and without the need for conscious reasoning. It is a knowing, which we are not able to explain through any logical explanations. It, in fact, opens the door wide open for the metaphysical aspect of mankind – the tool that we connect with to our soul.

What is Frequency? What is Vibration?

In simple terms, a frequency is the rate per second (or any other unit of measurement) of a vibration that constitutes a wave. Vibration, on the other hand, is the oscillating or other periodic motion of a rigid or elastic body forced from a position or state of equilibrium.

In chemistry, lecturers teach that literally everything is made up of atoms, which are in a constant state of motion. Therefore, depending on the speed of these vibrations, things appear as solid, liquid, or gas. The sound is a vibration, and thoughts (as discussed in Chapter 17) are brainwaves and, as they oscillate at different frequencies, they get classified in bands such as alpha, theta, and gamma. These brainwaves allow our brain cells to tune into the frequency that corresponds to their particular task. Hence, science produces strong evidence that listening to music can positively impact the brain's health and function.

Everything that manifests itself in your life, exists in your life because it matches with the vibration of your thoughts. This concept is analogous to the famous law of attraction: Like attracts like. We live in a system of natural Divine laws, which operates sans any prejudices, racisms, or discriminations. When the sun is out on one side of the earth, it shines its light equally upon everything that exists. Similarly, our inner life dictates our external life, and the very fabric of this reality is designed to mirror to us this inner life so we can, in turn, reveal our true essence.

We are all Made of Elements

Almost every living thing on Earth is made up of four atomic elements: oxygen, carbon, hydrogen, and nitrogen.

How do we categorize these elements?

1. **Fire: The root of the ego**

   Fire is considered and proven to be the first element created when the universe was produced by the big explosion, which the science calls the Big Bang Theory. The fire has the attributes to transform, purify as well as destroy. On the physical plane, which is called the Earth, fire is symbolized by the sun, it gives warmth, and enables life. On the spiritual plane, fire stands for light. Fire symbolizes incredible energy that is hard to control, as well as activity, creativity, passion, freedom, love, anger, strength, will, courage, etc.

2. **Air: The lack of depth and commitment phase of the ego**

   Air is associated with the breath of life (in Genesis 2:7, God breathed into Adam's nostrils the breath of life) and it symbolizes creativity, imagination, knowledge, communication, travel, and more. This element of life can also shape into a force of terrible destruction, for example, in the case of cyclones.

3. **Water: The pleasure phase of the ego**
   Water has the power of cleansing, it is life-giving, and it can also be as destructive as the other elements. Therefore, it symbolizes death as well as rebirth, fluidity, stability, purification, strength, regeneration, change, and more.

4. **Earth: The depression or moodiness phase of the ego**
   The Earth element is the ultimate feminine principle of the universe. Mother Earth is constantly undergoing transformation and indicates the origin as well as the end of everything. It symbolizes fertility, nourishment, groundedness, strength, permanence, abundance, and more.

The above sequence of the elements provides you – the reader – a roadmap to follow, in order for you to optimally introspect and achieve a realization of your current stage with each of your desires. Every desire originates from our fiery nature (the ego). When we are unable to master our desires, they mutate to follow any of these phases, depending on your choices.

There is also a 5th element, called the aether, which is a mysterious force and signifies our spirit.

These four elements rule the 12 zodiac signs as well as the cosmos. The diverse elemental properties have been associated with behavioral attributes and personalities of individuals. Therefore, individuals, who are born under a particular zodiac sign are believed to have characteristics similar to that of the element governing their sign.

Because we are made of the same elements as this entire universe, how can we be separate? And if we are all made of the same elements, don't they influence us as much as we influence them?

As detailed in Chapter 1: Psychology, the Science of the Soul, we concluded that we are unable to use the word "science" to study the soul or the metaphysical aspects of mankind. Science is categorized by its study, observations, experiments, and facts given in experiences and the laws that govern them. While the notion of the soul is metaphysical and immortal from the spiritual and moral life, we can observe in it the supernatural and the free principle that escapes measurements and sets of statistical numbers. However, we are able to say that psychology is the atypical science of the soul.

During the nineteen-nineties, Dr. Masaru Emoto performed a series of experiments, wherein he observed the physical effect of words, thoughts, intentions, prayers, music, and environment on the crystalline structure of water. In addition, in the last decade, much research has been conducted on how water has memory and that it is influenced by our thoughts and intentions. One of the known experiments was conducted by Dean Radin, Ph.D., who is the Chief Scientist at IONS (Institute of Noetic Sciences) and Adjunct Faculty in the Department of Psychology at Sonoma State University. With him, as co-investigators, were Dr. Masaru Emoto, a Japanese energy scholar and author, and a few other researchers and scientists. The experiment proposed to measure how intention affects water crystal formation.

They wanted to test the hypothesis, that the exposure of water to distant intentions affects the aesthetic shapes of ice crystals formed in that water post the exposure. For a period of three days, approximately 2,000 people in Germany and Austria focused their intentions towards water samples placed inside an electromagnetically shielded chamber in California, while some other samples were placed outside of the shielded room.

A technician photographed ice drops formed from multiple samples of this same water that was submitted to these different treatment conditions. Each image was assessed for aesthetic beauty by over 2,500 independent judges. In the final stage of the experiment, different individuals, with no prior information about the actual experiment, analyzed the results of the data. The results proved that the test was consistent with a number of previous studies, thereby suggesting that intentions are able to influence the structure of water.

Correspondingly, in the recent years, several experiments have been conducted to demonstrate quantum entanglement, which means that two or multiple particles are intersected in such a way that the measurement of one particle's quantum state determines the possible quantum states of the other particles. This connection is not dependent upon the location of the particles in space. Thus, we can correspondingly suggest that our consciousness, which is our coherent quantum field of information, can become entangled with that of water and possess the ability to influence its structure.

As a fetus, we spend nine months floating in water in our mother's womb. This mystical element, which can exist in different states (liquid, solid, or gas) enables life and it is one of the first manifestations of the Light at the beginning of creation. Therefore, if human thoughts and intentions can significantly impact water, just imagine its effects on us, our environment, and the collective subconsciousness that influences us as a whole! Remember, the human body is made of 73% water and so is Earth covered with 71% of water!

Everything Influences Everything

"Love thy neighbor as thyself" (Mark, 12:31) is the most important and impactful Commandment. When I love my neighbor, I also love myself, because we are not separate. Separation is part of the design of the physical world, and our ego magnifies it. However, to be able to love the neighbor as myself, I need first to begin to love myself. Notably, only when we begin to love ourselves, we stop craving a different life, and we can see that everything that surrounds us is propelling and inviting us to grow. It is imperative to remember that we can't receive what we can't give. However, to be able to achieve that, we need to understand how our individual psyche function. As well as, to recognize that the pilot of our body is – **the ego** – which directs our lives subconsciously when we are not self-aware and in control of our own reactivities, reflexes, actions, and so on.

My desire is that everyone is able to recognize that our psyche can disturb us and it can make us sick. **However, as we connect it to the soul, the ego then, transforms into a valuable ally.** You have now a book in your hands detailing the characteristics as well as, the components of the psyche to provide you – the reader – a clear and detailed roadmap. The primary objective is to assist you to peek into your inner life and unveil at least some of your blind spots. The only way that we can grow is when we are aware of ourselves, but, by following the path that society puts us through, we may not achieve this potential. The way societies are growing propelled by our egocentric aspects to mainstream everyone, is in turn, limiting the potential of our beings. We are all individually unique and amazing; the entire existence of humanity has already shown us that we all have a gift inside of us. The only difference is the ability to act on those gifts.

You Get Exactly What you Don't Want!

Because we live in a Universe based on laws, if you actively don't want something, it will simply manifest in your life. The only way to remove the unwanted consists of recognizing its point of attraction in you and ceasing to feed this thought any of your energy. Let me reveal a secret – one that is very important to this reality and a kind of complex concept to grasp: **In this physical reality, we are the mirror!**

Inside of this giant mirror, we have absolutely no control or influence, because it is governed by the natural laws. However, outside of it, in the non-physical dimension, we have full control. It is from where we derive our consciousness and where the inner intention turns into a point of attraction to manifest to the outer intention, i.e. in the physical reality. Consequently, to step out of the mirror, one needs to refocus their individual attention on the image in front of that mirror and the corresponding attitudes towards it, which originates from the "inner world." Thus, this implies to forego the focusing on the reflection itself, which consist of the external reality conditions (environment), where each atom of these conditions are conspiring to help the individual refocus and thus, become consciously self-aware to manifest what would serve the spiritual growth.

However, there is a ruse in this movie of life, "The Giant Mirror." The ego will beguile you to see what it wants you to see. **Yes, it will!** In Chapter 17, we discussed how the ego resolves such frustrations by creating explanations for our behavior and physically rewriting it in our memories through memory reconsolidation. Thus, it deceives us into believing that we were in control of our actions. The ego's perception of reality is always tailored and aligned with the individual psychological states, extracted directly from the subconscious. Our consciousness is limited in not granting a direct access to the subconscious in our waking state like this invisible power, the ego. Therefore, you actually see what benefits its survival.

When you are self-aware and able to recover the aspects of yourself, which present the need of recovery, the ego will no longer be able to use those for its benefit, as they become parts of your awakened consciousness. Thus, your perception of the same things undergoes a change. In Sartre's description of emotion, we have discussed that **it is the body that is directed by consciousness, which changes its relations to the world so that the world changes our own qualities.** Remember, the ego also is a part of our consciousness as well as all that constitutes the "Me," and so thus it is all my identity and in fact, not the soul's. Now, should you experience an internal resistance in receiving this very important concept, we shall go on detailing it further and open for you the secret door to your own self.

To start with, would you be able to answer this question, as posed by Plato: **"How can you prove whether at this moment we are sleeping, and all our thoughts are a dream; or whether we are awake, and talking to one another in the waking state?"**

We have discussed in Chapter 14 the nature of dreams through the psychological perspectives. We learned that all psychic consciousness can be ascribed to the mind, and the subconscious can be ascribed to the soul. We can attribute our dreams to our soul, which travels through the non-physical dimensions. Our minds do not imagine dreams but actually perceives them. The human soul has direct access to the astral or non-physical dimensions. However, as long as we are not consciously aware of being asleep, we are absorbed in the unconscious dream and thus unable to control the happenings around us. But the moment the dreamer is able to consciously realize he/she is dreaming and subsequently acknowledge their relation to the physical reality, it projects a revelation of some breathtaking abilities pertaining to that dimension. The improved psyche allows you to perform astonishing manifestations with an optimal use of the power of your intention. (For example, flying: The moment you think of a place, pouf! You are there, instantly!) As Carl Jung said, "The dream is a little hidden door in the innermost and most secret recesses of the soul, opening into that cosmic night which was psyche long before there was any ego-consciousness, and which will remain psyche no matter how far our ego-consciousness extends."

Let us now consider that one morning you wake up on this side of the mirror in the physical reality – but, in fact, you are dreaming. You go on with your daily life events, while you perceive each of them with a new perspective. The experience is as if you have broken out of the continuum of time-space and found yourself simultaneously a part of this reality and, as well, separate from it. This is exactly analogous to what happens when you consciously dream and realize the dream actually depends on your consciousness (and that it will be out of your control when dreaming subconsciously). Similarly, living on this side of the mirror while grasping the concept that we are dreaming but awake is just the same, too. The only difference is that this physical reality doesn't react as quickly as the non-physical (for the reasons we have discussed previously the fabric of space-time, which exists to serve as a continuum for life experiences and allows a space-time between the cause and the effect). Otherwise, we would not have a need to choose. For example, if you slap someone, you instantly receive a slap back... although not by whom you have just slapped, but by this invisible balancing force on this side of the mirror, which we call life. Would you ever dare to slap anybody after that? I am sure you would think 100 times before repeating such an act!

The fabric of space-time is a by-product of our inherited free will. Without our free will, we would be living in a kind of enslaved static state, which is definitely not as exciting! Don't you agree?

Now, the moment you understand and learn the operative mechanism of time-space delay on the side of our physical reality, you will discover amazing things. Like, how much reality is infinitely flexible, infinitely full of potentials, and infinitely changeable. In order to demonstrate this with an example, imagine a very unusual situation: You stand in front of a mirror and you can't see your own reflection. Then, minutes later, an image of you appears. You tilt your head, in wonder of the lagging you have just experienced. However, in the mirror, the same image remains of you, standing with your head upright. That is just exactly how the Universe operates; only the time-space laws that manifest our intentions are far greater and beyond the grasp of our narrow human consciousness.

As soon as you can rewire your brain neurons to perceive reality, in the actual form, you will learn to tune into your intuition much more, and your every thought would stem from the best intentional places, i.e. from within your core being.

In consequence, what does this entirely mean to you? Where would you be standing right at that moment? **You are standing outside of this physical reality by tuning into your own soul** – you have stepped outside that giant mirror. Indeed, you started to create consciously the life, which you truly desire from the other side. And this, in turn, will reflect back to you on this side.

Live Authentically

Within each one of us, there is a magnificent radiant power: The soul. When we learn how to really connect with ourselves, we comprehend and possess the true freedom of being. It is through this freedom that we are able to create authenticity in our lives. It comes from this deep and infinite space inside of us. Specifically, this area is from where you extract your true self and transcend your ego.

I wish I could tell that you will be able to live a life without challenges, but I cannot surely promise that. To be alive is to encounter life challenges and so, without this very powerful and sophisticated tool, how do you expect to outgrow yourself? If there is nothing in you that needs to be outgrown and progress, how do you expect to reveal the Light of the Creator and your own Light? (If there was only light, would a candlelight make any difference next to the sunlight?)

Despite that, we are no longer the united power, which in old days used to move heaven and earth. This indicates the collective subconscious deafening screams, through which all our souls call out for the gates of Heaven to open and pour more mercy over mankind. Humanity remains to be that strong will to seek, which is driven by our essence that is already whole. It brings to the forefront the soul, which is more magnificent, beautiful, and gigantic than we can possibly imagine. We are perfect and we are complete. But, we have forgotten who we are, and have disconnected ourselves from the source of life (the Creator). This huge blunder, which has impacted us deeply, is attributed to this feeling of separation **created by the fiery ego.** We allowed it to dictate and run our lives. Each one of us is capable of giving infinite love from our individual infinite well. However, we see so much lack of love around us. Therefore, our way back home can only be achieved through being increasingly self-aware, loving ouselves and others as thyself. As well as, by embodying the spirituality to start revealing the Light of the Creator in this physical reality, and by elevating this material world to a new earth.

We have all, just like an onion, developed layers that we hide behind. However, the time has come for each one of us to start peeling off those layers, in order to impact a revelation to the world of our authentic selves – a luminous, magnificent, and loving soul.

As Carl Jung stated, **"The world will ask you who you are, and if you do not know, the world will tell you."**

He also said, **"I am not what happened to me, I am what I choose to become."**

PARTING WORDS FROM THE AUTHOR

A life lived without knowing your inner self or spirituality is like being on a plane without fuel. You can live in it for a very long time; however, you are not going to go far.

Therefore, my biggest desire is that we all make conscious and good choices. Being conscious means that you are aware that each behavior, decision, thought and anything you say has an effect – either negative or positive.

Ultimately, which side of these polarities you connect with is always your choice!

"Out of suffering have emerged the strongest souls; the most massive characters are seared with scars."

Said by the Lebanese writer and poet Kahlil Gibran

ABOUT THE AUTHOR

 Rémi Meyer was born in Beirut, Lebanon and later on moved to Cyprus where he spent a big part of his life. Rémi spent his childhood, growing up under the influence of Catholic nuns at a French school he attended. Despite it being a Catholic school and possessing its own church on premises, the nuns welcomed all type of beliefs. They had a progressive secular outlook in uniting people.

Rémi's unfortunate childhood was fraught with several years of emotional and physical abuse. The adverse circumstances were created by none other than his own mother, sadly – a good woman who was not taught better. As a youngster, he was able to acutely perceive and understand the abusive patterns and emotional manipulation caused by his mother. She put him and his siblings through the worse, and because he was born with heightened empathic abilities, he could discern the atrocities.

He was downhearted that the very exact place where he was supposed to feel safe at home, he was not. He realized that there was something troubling about the way he and his siblings were treated. Until, gradually, as the time progressed, he was able to understand the reasons underpinning his mother's behaviors. This living amongst an abusive family and a culture built on abusive approach was an intense period in his life. However, despite being raised in an extremely painful environment, Rémi always felt the undeniable and unconditional love the Creator continues to hold for this entire universe.

Holding compassion towards others, Rémi has an innate ability to pierce into the psyche and emotional states of people around him. However, this gift, concurrently caused Rémi great frustration, as he could perceive that the majority of people's behaviors is subconsciously propelled primarily by their "ego self." In these delusive conditions him great pain and grief.

Being uniquely different from his family and possessing special observational skills brought forward in Rémi an unquenched thirst for understanding the sophistication of the human psyche. He looked for answers through the lens of psychology, psychoanalysis, philosophy, sociology, anthropology, biology and metaphysics. He has been researching and studying these subjects in depth for the last 20 years. This helped Rémi understand the reasons that dictate each and every conduct – his, and those of others.

Holding a very special place in his heart, Cyprus offered Rémi the serenity he needed with space and time to self-reflects on his childhood and life. The magnetic pull he feels towards the island is always present in him. He started his university studies and subsequently transferred to the United States to complete his studies at the University of Indianapolis, IN. He graduated in 2006, and then moved back to the island, where he pursued a successful career. He has also received a Medal of Honor and Courage for the volunteer work he did for the French Government (he helped expatriate European nationals from Lebanon to Cyprus at the time of war). He has, in addition, worked in Business Development arena, which offered him the privilege to travel frequently all over Europe and sometimes the world.

During his life, Rémi has lived in seven countries and has experienced the variety and diversity of cultures in these places. The travels and contacts he has had exposed him to a large spectrum of people from all corners of the world and thus offered him an expansive outlook on life. He has been quoted as saying, **"Whenever a person desires to experience** life on the intention of self-discovery; the entire universe will then conspire to assist that person. And, the more a person grows with those experiences, subsequently, the miracles of life surface. What actually changes are our outlooks, as well as our perceptions of things. Thus, those external things don't change – we do."

Rémi now lives in the United Kingdom, and he has made London his home for the last eight years. His passion and unquenched thirst to comprehend the sophistication of the human psyche still lives within him – and will, forever. His thirst for life and self-discovery will keep leading him on a journey of an infinite love to this extraordinary opportunity of existence – which we call life.

Printed in Great Britain
by Amazon